Leadership for the future
Nakka's Journey
To Organizational Excellence

VOLUME - 1

NAMO NARAYANA

INDIA • SINGAPORE • MALAYSIA

Dedication

To my teacher, who first showed me that every problem has a solution, who taught me the value of precision, patience, and perseverance.
Your lessons in mathematics became lessons in life,
and your belief in me laid the foundation for every step I've taken since.
Thank you for teaching me more than numbers,
for showing me the power of discipline, and for inspiring me to dream.

To the king, who, in ancient India, asked the profound question that transformed him into a Maharshi, reminding us of the eternal value of curiosity and inquiry.

To my friend, barge superintendent who taught me 5 secrete words to do any thing in life.

To my friend, dive superintendent who gave me the title as "Captain" (Captain Namo) for my performance as senior field engineer onboard.

To my two closest friends of 17 years, for your steadfast support, shared wisdom, and unwavering belief in me.

To the Telugu Veda Vyasa, who taught me to align my thoughts and emphasized the lasting importance of written words over fleeting visuals.

To my professor (Indian Institute of Technology, Kharagpur), who praised me for not asking a question while my classmate was asking very silly question.

To the UAE leadership, who gave an opportunity to learn visionary leadership from the books "My Vision: Challenges in the Race for Excellence" and "Reflections on Happiness and Positivity"

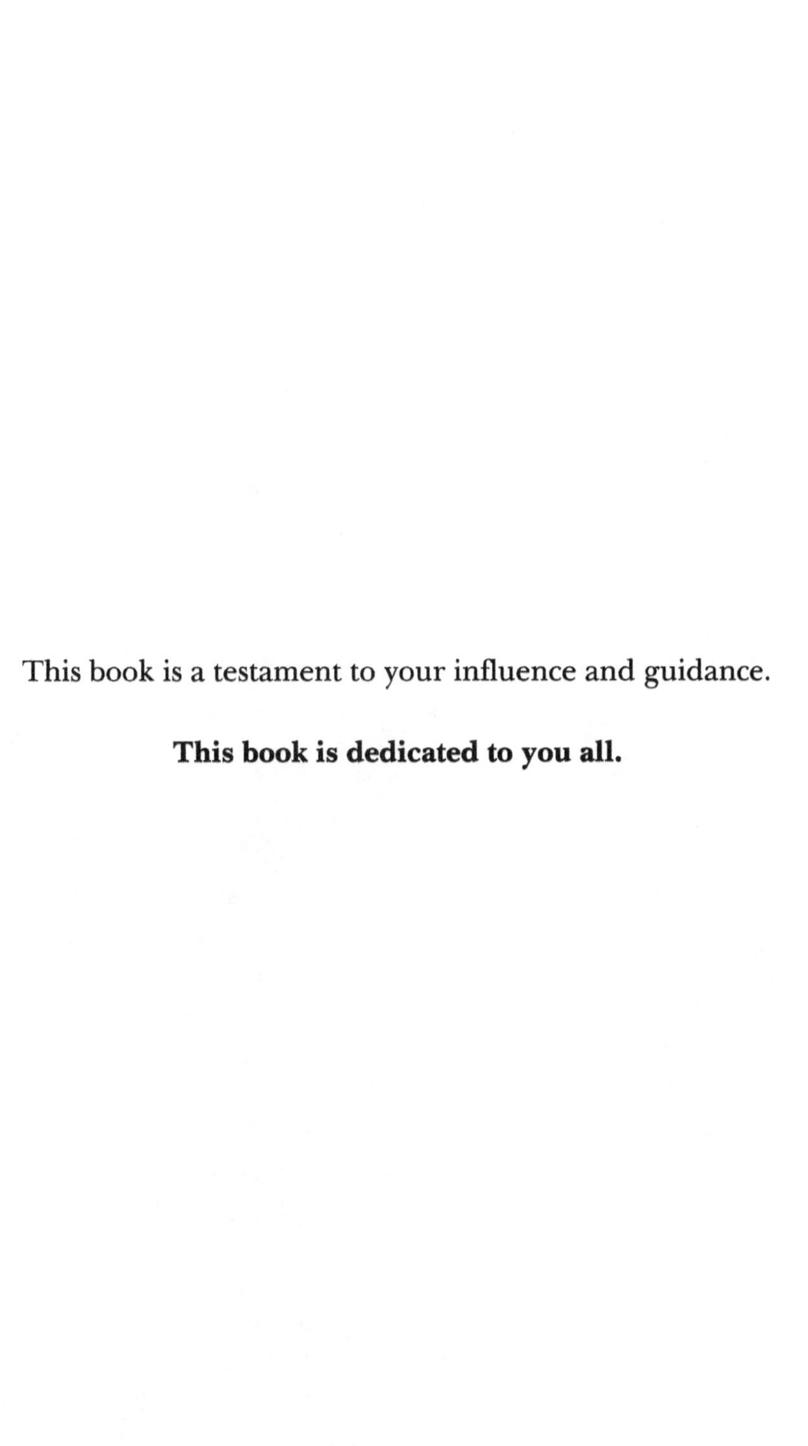

This book is a testament to your influence and guidance.

This book is dedicated to you all.

CONTENTS

PREFACE

As the author of *"Leadership for the Future: Nakka's Journey to Organizational Excellence,"* my inspiration for this book has been fueled by years of hands-on experience, challenges, and revelations within the fields of offshore and oil field construction engineering and leadership. Through my career, I've come to understand that the strength of any organization—whether a corporate entity, government body, or community-driven initiative—rests on its foundational values and the dedication of its people.

The story of Nakka is, in many ways, a reflection of the ideals, trials, and principles that I have encountered throughout my journey. Though fictionalized, Nakka's experiences embody the challenges of leading with integrity, resilience, and purpose, especially in environments that often prioritize immediate outcomes over long-term vision. I wanted to create a character who, like so many leaders I have met or aspired to be, finds his strength not in authority or control, but in values, wisdom, and the courage to face resistance with conviction.

This book was written for both emerging and seasoned leaders, for those who are committed to creating lasting impact through their work. It is a call to view leadership as an art that requires vision, empathy, and integrity—traits that are often seen as idealistic but are, in fact, essential to building a culture of trust, resilience, and excellence.

The principles in this book come from my observations and insights gained from years of engineering, management, and navigating complex organizational structures. In creating Nakka's journey, I have sought to present a story that is as much about the character's inner reflections as it is about his actions. I believe that leadership is, above all, a deeply personal journey, one that challenges us to align our inner values with the practical demands of the world around us.

My hope is that readers will find inspiration in Nakka's journey, that they will see parts of their own challenges in his experiences, and that they will come away with a renewed sense of purpose in their own leadership paths. Whether you lead a team of five or five hundred, the principles of clarity, ethics, wellness, and respect for individuals are universal. It is these principles that allow us to create organizations that do not just perform, but endure.

I extend my gratitude to the many mentors, colleagues, and friends who have shaped my understanding of leadership. Their insights have been invaluable in bringing this book to life. I am also grateful to the readers who take this journey with me through the pages of Nakka's story. May you find the wisdom here to lead with purpose, and the courage to make a difference.

Namo Narayana

ACKNOWLEDGMENTS

Writing *"Leadership for the Future: Nakka's Journey to Organizational Excellence"* has been a journey deeply intertwined with the wisdom, support, and encouragement of many remarkable individuals.

First and foremost, I am grateful to my mathematics teacher, whose influence inspired this dedication to lifelong learning and whose teachings continue to resonate within me. The clarity, patience, and precision instilled in those early years became the foundation of my pursuit of excellence.

To my mentors, colleagues, and friends in the fields of engineering, leadership, and organizational development—you have all contributed invaluable insights, encouragement, and constructive feedback. Your belief in the principles of integrity, purpose, and resilience has enriched every page of this book.

I also extend my heartfelt gratitude to my family, whose unwavering support has been my constant source of strength. Thank you for your patience, for understanding the late nights and early mornings, and for believing in the vision behind this work.

To every reader who picks up this book with the intention to learn, grow, and lead with integrity—this book is for you. May it inspire and empower you to create meaningful, lasting change.

Thank you all.
Namo Narayana

Book Introduction

THE PURPOSE OF NAKKA'S JOURNEY

In today's competitive landscape, leaders face a unique set of challenges. From balancing rapid growth with ethical practices to ensuring that employee well-being remains a priority, the responsibilities of leadership extend far beyond traditional notions of power and authority. This book, *"Leadership for the Future: Nakka's Journey to Organizational Excellence,"* is my contribution to that evolving conversation—a story that reveals not only the practical aspects of leadership but also the heart, conviction, and integrity required to truly inspire and sustain an organization.

The character of Nakka, although fictional, embodies the wisdom and lessons that have shaped my own career. Nakka's journey is about more than management—it's about building trust, creating lasting value, and leading with principles that honor both people and purpose. Each chapter explores different elements of organizational excellence, from clarity in roles and responsibilities to the importance of wellness and ethical integrity. The scenarios are intended to bring these lessons to life, to make them relatable and applicable across industries and roles.

This book is designed for anyone who seeks to make a positive impact through leadership, whether you are at the beginning of your career or already in a position of influence. I hope that you find Nakka's story as meaningful and inspirational as I have found the journey of writing it.

May this book offer you a fresh perspective on leadership, and may it empower you to create organizations that do not just function, but flourish.

NAKKA'S VISION AND THE SEEDS OF LEADERSHIP

Nakka's Journey Begins: The Origins of a Vision

Nakka did not set out to be a leader. In his earliest years, he had no particular interest in titles or authority. Instead, his life was marked by a fascination with principles, by a curiosity about what made people connect, succeed, and thrive. Growing up in a modest town, Nakka observed the world around him with a quiet intensity, noticing not just what people did but why they did it, what motivated their actions, and what sustained them through challenges.

From an early age, he found himself drawn to people who seemed to live with a sense of purpose, who moved through life not simply achieving but contributing to something larger than themselves. He came to see that true greatness was not in ambition alone but in commitment to values that endured. This realization planted the first seeds of what would become his leadership philosophy.

Success without purpose is empty, he would think to himself. *Achievement without principle is hollow.*

Nakka's journey was defined by this conviction—a belief that leadership was not merely about managing but about inspiring, about building with integrity, about creating something that would last.

An Encounter That Changed His Path

There was a pivotal moment in Nakka's youth that solidified his view of leadership. He remembered watching a local teacher, Mr. Rajan, guide a group of young students in building a community garden. Mr. Rajan was not the head of any large organization; he was simply a man dedicated to his work, to instilling values in those he taught. He led with quiet conviction, with respect for his students, with a belief in the value of hard work and care.

One day, Nakka asked Mr. Rajan why he dedicated so much time to the garden, why he cared so much for something that others saw as insignificant.

"Nakka," Mr. Rajan replied, "true leadership is not about telling others what to do. It is about showing them what is worth doing, about planting seeds—not only in the earth but in the heart. The garden may seem small, but the values it represents are vast. We are not here to create results alone; we are here to create meaning."

Those words stayed with Nakka, resonating deeply. He realized then that leadership was not about prestige; it was about purpose. It was about creating value, about leaving something behind that others could build upon, something that was both useful and meaningful.

The Roots of His Principles

As Nakka's career began, he entered the corporate world not to climb ladders but to understand systems, to learn what drove success and what created failure. He observed leaders who focused only on profit, on results, on metrics. And he saw others who led with vision, with a commitment to the well-being of their people, with a belief in the value of integrity. To Nakka, these differences were profound. He knew that leadership without purpose was fleeting, that organizations built only on ambition would falter when challenges arose.

True leadership is about principles, he thought. *It is about building with honor, with clarity, with a sense of responsibility that goes beyond the self.*

His principles began to take shape:

- **Integrity**: Nakka believed that integrity was the bedrock of trust, that without honesty and respect, no leader could hope to inspire or build loyalty.

- **Purpose**: To him, every action, every decision, every goal must be grounded in purpose. Achievement without meaning was merely vanity.

- **Empathy**: Nakka believed that leadership was about understanding, about seeing others as partners in a shared mission, about respecting the humanity of each person.

- **Resilience**: He understood that challenges were inevitable and that resilience was built not on force but on trust, on unity, on the strength of values.

These principles were not mere ideals; they were commitments, promises he made to himself and to the people he led.

Entering the Corporate World: Nakka's First Challenges

When Nakka first entered a formal leadership role, he was met with skepticism. His team was used to leaders who pushed for results, who measured success in numbers alone. They were not used to someone who asked about their well-being, who wanted to understand their challenges, who believed in purpose over performance metrics. At first, his team mistook his empathy for weakness, his commitment to integrity as an inability to drive results.

But Nakka knew that change would take time. He believed that to create something meaningful, he would have to earn trust, to demonstrate that values and success were not opposites but partners. His approach was not about forcing people to follow; it was about inviting them to see the value in his vision, to find their own purpose within the organization's mission.

A Vision for the Future: Building with Purpose and Integrity

As Nakka moved through his career, he grew increasingly convinced that organizations, like individuals, had a responsibility to lead with honor, to serve a purpose greater than profit alone. He wanted to create an environment where each person could thrive, where wellness, respect, and integrity were woven into the fabric of daily operations. To him, this was not idealism; it was practicality. He knew that people gave their best when they felt respected, when they believed in what they were building.

True success is not built in numbers; it is built in trust, in purpose, in the courage to do what is right.

Nakka's vision was clear: he wanted to lead an organization where principles were honored, where each person felt valued, where every decision was a reflection of integrity. He knew that such a vision required courage, that he would face resistance, that others might question his commitment to values over expediency. But he believed that true leadership was not about pleasing everyone; it was about staying true to what mattered.

Nakka's Legacy Begins

With each step forward, Nakka saw that he was not only building an organization; he was building a legacy, a testament to the power of leadership that prioritized values, that created meaning, that honored each person's humanity. He believed that an organization was not a machine but a community, a place where people could grow, could connect, could find purpose.

And so, Nakka's journey began—not as a quest for power but as a commitment to purpose, not as a path to wealth but as a mission to build something that would last, something that would inspire others to lead with courage, with honor.

He knew that his path would not be easy, but he also knew that it was worth walking. For Nakka, leadership was not a destination but a journey, a journey that began not with titles but with values, not with ambition but with purpose.

And with that vision in his heart, he stepped into the organization, ready to begin a journey that would change not only the lives of those he led but the very soul of the organization.

Chapter 1

THE FOUNDATION – ORGANIZATION CHART

Nakka's Resolve: A Structure for Vision and Purpose

Nakka stood at the edge of the conference room, eyeing the paper that had served as the company's organization chart. He traced its lines—the names and titles that crisscrossed the page, a flimsy attempt to capture the machine behind a rapidly growing company. Yet he knew the structure here was failing. This "chart" was no more than a formality, a compliance to tradition rather than a living guide that defined purpose and responsibility. He knew in that moment: a true organizational chart was not about hierarchy but about vision. It was a blueprint for clarity, for work that held meaning.

As Nakka studied the chart, his mind flashed back to a simpler scene. Years before, as a young engineer, he had seen how true clarity could shape outcomes. Back then, every piece of the structure had a purpose; every role knew its part, and there was no mistaking the line that connected ambition with reality. Here, ambition was fragmented, scattered across titles without weight.

Inwardly, he asked himself, *What does it take to make this structure breathe?*

The Rebuild

Nakka gathered the department heads around him, not for a meeting, but for a conversation—a deep, transformative exchange. As they sat, he could see in their eyes the weariness of leaders weighed down by invisible walls. Marketing clashed with Sales, Operations felt forgotten by Customer Service, and all felt directionless. They didn't need orders; they needed clarity.

"The roles you carry aren't mere titles," Nakka began, his voice steady yet resolute. "They are the building blocks of what this organization could be. A structure without purpose is dead. But a structure where each piece knows its purpose—that is power."

Silence followed as they digested his words. Then Saira, the head of Operations, spoke up, half skeptically.

"So, what? We're supposed to rewrite the whole system?" she asked. "We're already overwhelmed as it is."

Nakka saw in her question the resistance, a remnant of a system where people drifted through their roles without direction. He didn't respond immediately but let the question settle in the room. Finally, he replied, calm but forceful.

"Yes, Saira. But not just for the sake of change. We're rewriting it to bring life to what we do. If you walk out of this room not knowing what you stand for, then this company will fail. We'll rebuild it, not just on paper but in purpose."

Philosophical Underpinnings: The Organization as Identity

After that meeting, Nakka retreated into himself, contemplating the task ahead. He was alone, yet his thoughts vibrated with intensity, a conversation with his inner resolve. To Nakka, this was not just an organization—it was identity. Each title, each line in the chart was a declaration of accountability.

Structure is not limitation, he mused. *Structure is freedom—the freedom to know where you stand, to act within a space you understand.* Without it, ambition falls apart, scattered by forces that clash instead of unify.

He began drafting a new chart that night, not with boxes but with purpose statements. He was mapping out meaning, not just names. He knew that this new structure would serve as the company's foundation. Each role needed to reflect its purpose, its unspoken promise to the company's mission. The structure would guide each person, but it would also challenge them to bring more than just skill—to bring conviction.

A Dialogue on the Nature of Work

The next day, Nakka invited Rishi, the head of Sales, for coffee. Rishi had been with the company since the beginning, his sales numbers impressive, yet his methods chaotic. Nakka sensed that Rishi was uncomfortable with the rigid systems but also recognized his potential if he aligned with the company's broader vision.

"Rishi," Nakka began, stirring his coffee, "what does it mean to you, this job, this role you play here?"

Rishi shrugged, his usual confidence seeming to flicker for a moment. "It's a means to an end, isn't it? Hit the numbers, close the deals. That's my part. But sometimes I wonder if it even matters beyond the bottom line."

"You're wrong, Rishi," Nakka replied, his voice quiet but intense. "It matters profoundly. If you only see numbers, you're missing the foundation of your work. Those numbers are a result of the meaning we put into it. If we have no meaning, the structure we create crumbles. Do you understand?"

Rishi looked at him, his expression hard to read, but something in his eyes shifted.

"So, you're saying the structure gives us that meaning?"

"Not the structure itself," Nakka corrected. "But our commitment to it. When you understand your place in this structure—not as a limitation, but as a focus—you find purpose. You're not just Sales. You're the bridge to the outside world, the first impression of who we are. You define us to the world. That is your role. It is up to you to give it meaning."

The words resonated with Rishi in a way that no directive ever had. He saw his title in a new light, as a role connected to the identity of the entire organization.

Redefining the Organization Chart as a Blueprint for Identity

The new organization chart was unveiled a week later, but it was not just a chart; it was a manifesto. Each department had a statement of purpose beneath its title, a commitment to the company's mission.

Each role was defined not by task alone but by its impact, its relevance to the whole.

Marketing was no longer just a generator of leads; it was the voice that connected the organization's vision to the public. Operations was the steward of quality, ensuring that every product reflected the organization's values. Sales was the gateway, the first touchpoint that reflected the integrity of the entire operation. Every department, every title was imbued with purpose.

As he unveiled the chart, Nakka addressed the assembled employees, his voice filled with a conviction that was palpable.

"This is not just a piece of paper. This is our map. It is the architecture of our identity. You are not just filling a role; you are holding a place in something greater. If you do not understand this, if you do not bring meaning to it, then all of this falls apart. But if you choose to see it—to really see it—then you're part of something that can't be torn down."

There was silence, then a murmur, and finally a sense of quiet understanding. They were not just employees; they were creators, builders of an organization that demanded not just skill but purpose.

Philosophical Reflections: The Structure as Freedom

That night, Nakka sat in his office, alone with his thoughts. He felt the quiet satisfaction of someone who has built something meaningful. He knew this structure would be tested, challenged by those who saw it only as formality. But for Nakka, it was more than that. It was freedom.

To know your place within a larger whole, he reflected, *is not confinement—it is liberation. It allows you to act with certainty, to bring all of yourself to the role without hesitation. Without this foundation, our efforts scatter like dust. But with it... we are one force.*

Nakka understood then that he was not just creating a chart; he was creating a path, a way forward for those who believed that work could be more than just survival, that it could be purpose, that it could be life itself.

Key Takeaways from Nakka's Approach to the Organization Chart

1. **Structure as Purpose, Not Limitation**
2. Nakka redefined the organization chart not as a limitation but as a blueprint for identity. Each role was connected to a purpose beyond mere function.
3. **Individual Roles as Reflections of the Whole**
4. For Nakka, each role contributed to a unified identity. Employees were not separate entities but parts of a larger vision, each role essential in defining the organization.
5. **Clarity as a Path to Freedom**
6. Nakka believed that clarity in roles provided employees with freedom—the freedom to understand their place, to take ownership, and to contribute meaningfully.
7. **Purpose as the Foundation of Accountability**
8. By embedding purpose into each role, Nakka fostered accountability as something intrinsic, not imposed. Employees felt responsible to the structure because it represented more than just tasks; it represented their shared mission.

Legacy of Nakka's Foundation

In the months that followed, the organization transformed. Employees moved with a sense of purpose and direction. The organization chart, once a static piece of paper, became a living guide that they referred to with pride. They saw themselves in it, their place, their meaning.

Nakka's legacy was more than structure—it was purpose in motion. He had shown them that structure, when built on clarity and commitment, could elevate them, uniting individual ambitions into a force of shared purpose.

Chapter 2

THE VALUE OF DISCIPLINE – WORKING HOURS

Nakka's Insight: Time as a Reflection of Commitment and Integrity

The hum of the office lingered in the air as Nakka walked through the halls at dawn, well before the lights would flicker on. It was silent, and he found clarity in that silence—a sense of purpose that would soon be blurred by the chaos of the day. As the hours filled, the silence would dissolve into voices, movements, and decisions, each one carving away at time, each one either building toward or tearing from the company's purpose.

To Nakka, time wasn't merely a schedule; it was a commitment. He knew that how an organization managed its time—how individuals valued each hour—was a reflection of its deeper integrity. He saw employees trickling in late, meetings dragging on without end, and productivity slipping through the gaps in their schedules. The issue was not laziness, he knew. It was an absence of discipline, a lack of collective respect for the purpose that their time could serve.

Time is not just a resource, he mused. *Time is a promise—a promise to do something meaningful, something that justifies each hour.*

A Philosophy of Time: Nakka's Dialogue with Saira

Nakka sat down with Saira, the head of Operations, someone whose punctuality and attention to detail he admired. He wanted to discuss the larger question of time with her, to see if she too sensed the shift he felt was needed. He opened with a question that startled her.

"Saira, what do you think time means here, in this place, to all of us?"

Saira paused, caught off guard, but thoughtful. "It's... it's how we get things done, I suppose. Time is what we use to produce, to meet our targets. But sometimes, it feels as though we're just marking hours, clocking in and out without purpose."

Nakka nodded, his gaze intense. "That's precisely the problem. Time has to mean more than mere production. If we're just moving through it, marking it, we're not respecting it. We're not using it as a tool of integrity."

"So, what does that look like?" Saira asked, leaning forward, intrigued.

"Discipline," Nakka replied simply. "Discipline to honor time as if it were a contract—a contract not just with the company, but with ourselves. When we respect our hours, we build a foundation of reliability. Without that, every hour is a wasted chance at purpose."

Nakka could see a spark of understanding in her eyes, a shift as she considered his words. She nodded slowly, the beginnings of alignment between them forming, an unspoken agreement that time, when disciplined, became an expression of integrity.

A New Approach: Time as a Shared Commitment

Nakka knew that enforcing rigid hours wouldn't change anything on a deeper level. He wanted employees to internalize a commitment to their time, to see it not as a constraint but as a space within which they could bring purpose and focus. Rather than implementing stricter rules, he decided to cultivate an approach that emphasized flexibility paired with accountability. He set core hours—those few sacred hours during which everyone was expected to be present—and gave employees freedom outside of that to manage their time.

"Flexibility isn't an escape from discipline," Nakka explained in a company-wide meeting. "It's an invitation to trust. We trust you to honor your commitments, to meet your responsibilities with the freedom to choose how you do it. But understand this: without accountability, freedom is chaos. And we are not here to drift."

The words stirred something in the crowd. They had never heard time spoken of this way, as if each hour were a canvas, and they were the artists responsible for what would be painted on it.

Setting Boundaries to Preserve Focus

In the following weeks, Nakka introduced time-blocked schedules where each department would carve out blocks for uninterrupted work. Meetings were limited, purpose-driven, and set to end promptly. He worked closely with the team to streamline time use, ensuring that each hour spent in the office served a clear purpose. The days became structured but breathable, a rhythm of focus that made employees feel as though they were achieving something within each block of time.

He invited Rishi, the head of Sales, to a meeting to discuss the concept further.

"Rishi," Nakka said, "I want you to see your schedule not as a series of hours but as a series of commitments. Each block of time should reflect a goal, a purpose."

"So, I'm supposed to structure everything now?" Rishi replied, half-amused, half-resistant. "Time feels rigid as it is."

"Only if you think of it that way," Nakka replied, leaning forward, his tone growing intense. "Time is what you make of it. It can be a prison, or it can be a passage—a path toward something meaningful. Every hour you spend unfocused is an hour lost. But every hour spent with intention brings you closer to your purpose."

Rishi was quiet for a moment, the words settling deeply. In that silence, he understood: time was not about filling hours but about filling purpose. The commitment was his to make.

The Challenge of Reinforcement: Holding Each Other Accountable

As the weeks passed, Nakka saw the organization beginning to shift. There was a renewed sense of energy, a feeling that each person was taking ownership of their hours, of the work they put into them. But discipline, he knew, required more than mere intention; it required reinforcement. He introduced a peer accountability system, where each team member would pair with another, a "time partner," someone who could provide honest feedback on how effectively they were managing their time.

This, he believed, would make time a shared commitment, not an isolated act of self-discipline.

"If you respect your colleague's time as much as your own," he said to the team, "you will find yourself honoring each moment more consciously. Accountability is not just about meeting your goals—it's about respecting the space within which your colleagues work to meet theirs."

The concept took hold, and employees began to see time not just as individual hours but as collective progress. They became guardians of each other's purpose, reminders that each hour they worked was woven into the fabric of something larger.

Philosophical Reflection: The Essence of Disciplined Time

One evening, alone in his office, Nakka reflected on the changes he was beginning to see, but he also pondered the deeper meaning of what they were doing. To him, time discipline wasn't about rigid schedules or maximized output; it was about respect—for oneself, for the team, and for the work they were committed to.

Time is a canvas, he thought. *Each hour we choose to fill with purpose or let fall empty is a brushstroke that shapes not just our work but our legacy.*

In his mind, the organization was like a great river, moving purposefully in one direction. Each person's time was a current contributing to that movement. If one slacked or meandered, the flow faltered. But when each person worked with integrity, honored their hours, and contributed to the whole, the river was unstoppable.

The next day, he gathered the department heads once more.

"We have chosen to honor our time because it honors our purpose," he said, his tone filled with conviction. "If you want this organization to be more than a place where you spend your hours, then every day, choose to bring meaning to it. Let our time together be a testament to what we can build—not just in hours, but in purpose."

They left the room with something beyond new guidelines; they left with an invitation to see their work, and their time, as something sacred.

Key Takeaways from Nakka's Approach to Working Hours

1. **Time as Commitment, Not Constraint**
2. Nakka's philosophy transformed time from a limitation to a commitment. Each hour spent was a chance to build purpose, not merely fill a schedule.
3. **Flexibility with Accountability Fosters Trust and Discipline**
4. By pairing flexibility with accountability, Nakka allowed employees to manage their hours while ensuring each moment was respected, fostering a culture of mutual trust.
5. **Peer Accountability as Collective Ownership of Time**
6. Time partners reminded each employee that time was a shared commitment. This approach fostered a culture where each person felt responsible not only to themselves but to the team.
7. **Focus Time and Boundaries for Enhanced Productivity**
8. Time-blocking and limiting meetings created focus blocks, allowing employees to bring concentration and clarity to their work, leading to heightened productivity and satisfaction.
9. **Purpose-Driven Hours as a Path to Organizational Identity**
10. By treating time as a resource tied to purpose, Nakka shaped the organization's identity as one that valued integrity, discipline, and commitment to excellence.

Legacy of Nakka's Discipline

Months later, the organization felt transformed. Employees moved with a sense of purpose, each hour resonating with the echo of commitment. Time was no longer a passive passage; it had become an instrument of integrity. Nakka's discipline approach had elevated their work beyond routine, beyond schedules, into a realm where each hour held meaning, each commitment held weight. His legacy was not about hours saved, but about time respected—a lesson that would define them for years to come.

Chapter 3

DEPARTMENTS – THE PILLARS OF SPECIALIZATION

Nakka's Realization: Specialization Requires Collaboration to Create a Unified Force

Nakka stood at the balcony overlooking the office floor, where each department moved in its own rhythm. He watched as Marketing refined presentations, Sales closed deals, Operations managed schedules, and IT fixed lines of code. Each department was a self-sufficient unit, a world of its own, yet each depended on the others in ways they could not see.

To Nakka, this separation was both strength and weakness. Strength, because specialization created experts, individuals who excelled within their own realms. Weakness, because the silos had become walls, obstructing communication and stifling shared purpose. He knew that departments, if isolated, would never truly contribute to a single, united vision.

Specialization isn't about division, he thought. *It's about creating pillars that support a larger structure. If these pillars don't align, the structure collapses.*

The Challenge of Balance: Independence Within Interdependence

As Nakka walked down to the Operations department, he thought about how specialization often turned into isolation. Each team was so focused on its own goals that it had lost sight of the organization's broader mission. When he reached Saira, the head of Operations, he spoke with quiet intensity.

"Saira, how often do you talk to the Sales department?"

Saira raised an eyebrow, surprised by the question. "Not often enough, I suppose. We have our own timelines, our own responsibilities. If we're doing our jobs, we shouldn't need to coordinate with them too much."

"That's the problem," Nakka replied, his voice soft but firm. "If every department exists solely within itself, then we lose sight of what we're building together. Operations isn't just about schedules—it's about supporting Sales to deliver. And Sales isn't just about closing deals; it's about aligning with Marketing to communicate our vision. We are each part of something larger."

Saira listened, the weight of his words settling in. She saw now that Operations wasn't just about efficiency; it was about creating a foundation on which other departments could excel.

Defining Each Department's Purpose and Role

Over the following weeks, Nakka worked with each department head to define the unique purpose each team served within the organization. But he didn't stop there. He wanted each department to understand not only their purpose but the purpose of those around them, to see the organization as a symphony, where every instrument had its role but where harmony was essential.

Steps to Define Departmental Purpose:

1. **Crafting Purpose Statements for Each Team**
2. Nakka held sessions with department leaders, helping each team craft a purpose statement. Marketing's statement was to "connect the organization's vision with the world." Operations aimed to "build a foundation of reliability." Each purpose aligned with the organization's larger mission but allowed for the individuality of each department.
3. **Establishing Cross-Departmental Workshops**
4. Nakka introduced workshops where departments met to discuss their roles, their goals, and the ways in which they intersected.

These workshops weren't merely meetings—they were dialogues, spaces where departments could align their efforts.

5. **Fostering Respect for Each Team's Expertise**
6. He wanted departments to understand and respect each other's expertise. Each team brought something unique to the organization, a specialization that was essential. He encouraged teams to recognize that these differences made them stronger, that specialization created a robust support system for shared goals.

A Dialogue on Purpose with Rishi from Sales

Nakka approached Rishi once again, intrigued by the Sales department's unique position as the bridge between the company and the external world. Rishi was focused, results-driven, yet he often viewed Marketing and Customer Service as distant, unrelated worlds.

"Rishi, what does Sales mean to you?"

Rishi shrugged, thoughtful but direct. "It's about hitting targets, bringing in revenue. We keep the company alive, in a way."

"And what about Marketing?" Nakka pressed.

Rishi paused. "They generate leads, sure. But we don't interact much. They do their part, we do ours."

"But don't you see?" Nakka replied, his voice intense with conviction. "Sales is the voice of Marketing, the bridge between our message and the customer. If you don't see yourself in partnership with Marketing, you're only selling a product—not a vision."

Rishi looked at him, the words resonating. Nakka had given him a glimpse of something deeper, a realization that Sales wasn't just about numbers. It was about representing the entire organization to the world, a responsibility that required collaboration, not isolation.

Creating Mechanisms for Cross-Departmental Collaboration

Nakka knew that understanding each other's purpose was just the beginning. Departments needed tangible ways to work together, to integrate their specialized skills into a unified force. He introduced cross-departmental projects and teams, each one designed to bridge gaps and foster shared purpose.

Approaches to Foster Cross-Departmental Collaboration:

1. **Cross-Functional Project Teams**
2. Nakka formed project teams that included members from multiple departments, encouraging each team to bring its expertise to a single goal. These projects became models of what the organization could accomplish when departments worked as one.
3. **Regular Interdepartmental Meetings**
4. He instituted regular interdepartmental meetings, where department heads shared updates, discussed challenges, and aligned their efforts. These meetings were structured to create dialogue, not mere reporting, allowing for real-time feedback and adjustments.
5. **Integrated Performance Metrics**
6. To reinforce interdependence, Nakka introduced metrics that tied department success to shared outcomes. Marketing, Sales, and Customer Service, for example, shared goals related to customer satisfaction, encouraging them to see themselves as part of a larger cycle rather than isolated functions.

Philosophical Reflection: Specialization as Unity

Alone in his office that evening, Nakka thought deeply about the nature of specialization. It struck him that departments, like people, needed purpose. They needed to know that their work mattered, that their specialization was not a detachment but a connection. Specialization, he realized, was unity when aligned with a common purpose.

Specialization is a paradox, he thought. *It divides us into roles, yet, when rightly understood, it is what binds us together. Each department, each role, is a pillar. And only when all pillars support one another can the organization rise.*

The organization he envisioned was one where each team contributed uniquely, yet in harmony with the others. It was a structure that was not merely functional but alive, each part resonating with purpose.

The Unveiling of a Collaborative Framework

The following month, Nakka unveiled a new framework for collaboration. It was more than a strategy; it was a philosophy of unity through specialization. Each department's purpose statement was posted on a board in the main hall, a reminder of the role each played within the greater whole.

"This," Nakka said to the assembly, "is not just a strategy. It is a testament to what we believe in—that specialization is not isolation but integration. If you see yourself only within your department, you miss the meaning of your work. But if you see your work as part of the whole, you find something greater than task or title. You find purpose."

The room was silent as his words sank in. They saw themselves, for the first time, not just as departments but as interconnected parts of a single entity. Each person felt a renewed sense of importance, of belonging. Their specialization was their gift to the organization, but their collaboration was what made it whole.

Key Takeaways from Nakka's Approach to Departments

1. **Specialization Requires Purpose to Avoid Isolation**
2. Nakka emphasized that specialization without a shared purpose led to silos. By defining each department's purpose, he gave specialization meaning, linking it to the organization's vision.
3. **Cross-Departmental Collaboration Fosters Unity Through Diversity**
4. Through cross-functional projects and regular meetings, Nakka bridged the gaps between departments, turning specialization into a source of strength rather than division.
5. **Integrated Performance Metrics Encourage Collective Responsibility**
6. By tying performance metrics to shared goals, Nakka encouraged departments to support one another's success, reinforcing a culture of collaboration.
7. **Specialization as a Foundation for Identity**

8. Nakka saw each department as a unique pillar of the organization. By aligning these pillars, he created an identity that was unified yet diverse, a structure where each team's role was valued and essential.

Legacy of Nakka's Vision for Specialization

In the years that followed, the organization flourished. Departments that once saw themselves as isolated worlds became collaborators, partners in a journey toward a shared mission. Employees moved with a sense of purpose, their work interwoven into a structure that was both specialized and unified.

Nakka's legacy was more than a framework; it was a belief, a conviction that specialization, when aligned with purpose, could create unity. He had shown them that their differences, their unique strengths, were not divisions but bonds. And in that unity, they found strength, purpose, and an organization that could withstand any challenge.

Chapter 4

ACCOUNTABILITY THROUGH CLARITY – ROLES & RESPONSIBILITIES

Nakka's Conviction: Clarity as the Path to Ownership

Nakka leaned back in his chair, his gaze fixed on the ceiling as he contemplated the nature of responsibility. The organization was thriving, yet he sensed something elusive—an invisible line between effort and purpose that his team struggled to cross. They worked hard, each carrying a title, a description, a role, yet he could see hesitation in their actions. There was a reluctance to take full ownership, as if the boundaries of their responsibilities were blurred by uncertainty.

Clarity is freedom, Nakka thought. *To know one's role, one's boundaries, is to be empowered. But when those lines are invisible, accountability dissolves.*

He knew then that roles and responsibilities needed to be more than words on paper. They had to be anchors, symbols of commitment, so clear that each person would feel compelled to own their place in the organization, not merely perform it.

A Dialogue on Ownership with Maya, Head of Marketing

Nakka invited Maya, the head of Marketing, to his office for an honest discussion. She was brilliant, capable, but he sensed that she, too, felt the pull of ambiguity in her role. Marketing was both broad and vital, a department responsible for shaping the organization's identity in the public eye, yet she often hesitated when faced with decisions that crossed into the realm of Sales or Operations.

"Maya, what does 'ownership' mean to you?" Nakka asked, his tone contemplative.

Maya looked thoughtful, hesitant. "It's… taking charge, I suppose. Making decisions, moving forward."

"Yes, but ownership is also about clarity. It's about knowing that this responsibility is yours, and yours alone. Without that clarity, do you truly feel ownership?"

Maya's expression shifted, a glimmer of understanding sparking in her eyes. "I suppose not. Sometimes, I don't act because I'm not sure where my responsibility ends, where someone else's begins."

"Precisely," Nakka said, leaning forward. "If you don't have clarity, you can't act with confidence. Responsibility becomes fragmented, and action is lost in hesitation. Maya, when you know the boundaries of your role—when they are clear—you are free to own it completely, to make it yours."

Maya nodded, the weight of his words settling deeply. She realized then that clarity wasn't just structure; it was permission. It was the authority to act with conviction.

The Path to Clarity: Defining Roles with Purpose

Nakka understood that clarity in roles was a journey, one that required each person to see their responsibilities not as tasks, but as commitments. He initiated a series of workshops to refine the definitions of roles, working with each department to create role clarity documents. These were not just job descriptions; they were declarations of purpose, statements that linked each role to the organization's vision.

Steps to Create Role Clarity:

1. **Revisiting the Core Purpose of Each Role**
2. Nakka held discussions with every department head, challenging them to define each role's purpose. It was a process of distillation, stripping away tasks that didn't contribute to the core mission and enhancing those that did.
3. **Defining Decision-Making Authority and Boundaries**

4. For each role, Nakka outlined the scope of decision-making authority. He wanted each person to know not only what they were responsible for but what they had the power to decide. It was a liberation, allowing them to act without hesitation, to feel that their role carried weight.

5. **Linking Responsibilities to Organizational Goals**

6. Nakka didn't just define roles; he connected each one to the organization's larger mission. He wanted employees to see their roles as part of a greater whole, each responsibility contributing to a unified vision.

An Exchange on Accountability with Raj, Head of Finance

One afternoon, Nakka met with Raj, the head of Finance, who had been grappling with issues of accountability within his team. Raj's department was vital to the organization's stability, yet he often found his team deferring decisions to him, afraid to take responsibility for their actions.

"Raj, why do you think your team hesitates to make decisions?" Nakka asked, his voice calm but probing.

Raj sighed. "They're afraid of making mistakes. They don't want to take the blame if something goes wrong."

Nakka nodded thoughtfully. "That's because they don't feel true ownership. Responsibility without ownership is empty—it creates fear. But if they know that this role, this decision, is theirs to make, they will act not out of fear but out of purpose."

"So, how do I change that?" Raj asked, genuinely curious.

"Give them the boundaries," Nakka replied, his eyes intent. "Define their roles so clearly that there is no room for hesitation. When they know that a decision is within their realm, they will own it. They will become accountable because they have been given the authority to act."

Raj understood. The clarity Nakka spoke of was not restriction; it was empowerment. To be given boundaries was to be given the freedom to move within them, to take risks, to innovate.

Building a Culture of Ownership

Nakka's goal was not simply to create a structure of accountability; he wanted a culture where each person felt that their role was a personal commitment, a space they owned within the organization. He introduced a feedback loop where employees could review their roles with managers, discussing their responsibilities and seeking clarity on any ambiguities. This was a dynamic process, a living system that encouraged growth and adaptability.

Methods to Foster Ownership Through Role Clarity:

1. **Regular Feedback Sessions**
2. Nakka encouraged managers to hold regular one-on-one meetings with employees, discussing not just tasks but their understanding of their role and responsibilities.
3. **Decision-Making Workshops**
4. He introduced decision-making workshops where employees learned to navigate their roles, identifying when to act independently and when to seek input. This empowered them to take ownership without hesitation.
5. **Annual Role Audits**
6. Each role was reviewed annually to ensure it aligned with the organization's evolving needs. This process kept responsibilities relevant, preventing stagnation and fostering growth.

Philosophical Reflection: Clarity as Freedom

As he sat alone in his office, Nakka reflected on the journey he was undertaking. To him, clarity was a gift. It was the antidote to doubt, the remedy for hesitation. When roles were defined, when responsibilities were clear, people could act with confidence, with conviction. They could bring their full selves to their work, knowing that they were not just filling a position but embodying a purpose.

Clarity is the pathway to freedom, he thought. *When we know where we stand, we are free to move. When we know our role, we are free to commit.*

He realized that accountability wasn't something that could be enforced; it was something that had to be inspired. Each person had to feel that their role was theirs to own, a space where they could bring purpose, where they could make a difference.

The Power of Clear Roles in Action

In the months that followed, the impact of role clarity was profound. Employees moved with a sense of direction, of purpose. Decisions were made without hesitation, tasks completed without constant oversight. The organization felt alive, each part working in harmony with the others, a symphony of commitment.

One day, Nakka walked past a group of employees discussing their roles with a sense of ownership he had not seen before. They spoke not of tasks but of impact, of how their work contributed to the organization's vision. He saw in their faces the freedom he had envisioned—a freedom born not of autonomy alone but of clarity, of knowing exactly where they stood.

Key Takeaways from Nakka's Approach to Role Clarity

1. **Clarity in Roles as a Foundation for Ownership**
2. Nakka believed that people could only truly own their work if their roles were clear. By defining responsibilities, he gave employees the freedom to act with confidence and commitment.
3. **Boundaries as Empowerment**
4. For Nakka, boundaries weren't restrictions; they were permissions. By establishing decision-making authority, he empowered employees to make decisions without fear, creating a culture of accountability.
5. **A Culture of Growth Through Feedback and Adaptability**
6. Nakka's feedback loop kept roles dynamic, ensuring that responsibilities evolved with the organization's needs, fostering adaptability and continuous improvement.
7. **Clarity as the Path to Purpose**

8. Role clarity allowed employees to see their work as part of a greater mission, turning tasks into commitments, and creating a culture where each role held meaning.

Legacy of Nakka's Vision for Accountability

Years later, the organization thrived as a model of ownership and responsibility. Employees at every level felt that their work mattered, that their role was more than a title. They had found purpose in clarity, freedom in boundaries, and pride in accountability. Nakka's legacy was not a rigid structure but a culture where clarity inspired commitment, where roles were not just filled but lived, each one a reflection of purpose.

Nakka had shown them that true accountability was not a demand; it was a gift—a gift that empowered them to bring their fullest selves to the work, knowing that they belonged, that their place in the organization was not just defined but valued.

Chapter 5

LEVERAGING TECHNOLOGY – ENGINEERING SOFTWARE

Nakka's Realization: Tools Alone Do Not Build Mastery

The hum of computer monitors and the quiet tap of keyboards filled the office as Nakka moved through the engineering department. He noticed the advanced software running on each screen, programs capable of complex calculations, models that simulated real-world scenarios with precision. Yet, despite this sophisticated technology, projects were delayed, and errors persisted. He saw frustration in the engineers' faces, the disconnect between potential and reality.

To Nakka, technology was a tool—a powerful one, but only when wielded with understanding, with a mastery that transcended mechanics. He believed that technology was an extension of human skill, not a replacement for it. No software, however advanced, could substitute the insight, the precision, the intuition that came from human mastery.

Technology, without mastery, he thought, *is like a compass without direction. It may point, but it cannot guide.*

A Conversation with Alok, the Senior Engineer

Nakka invited Alok, one of the senior engineers, for a discussion. Alok was experienced, but he had become increasingly reliant on software outputs without questioning them, trusting the data without the scrutiny that expertise required.

"Alok," Nakka began, his tone gentle but probing, "do you feel that the software guides you, or do you guide it?"

Alok looked at him, confused. "I mean, the software does the calculations. We input the data, and it gives us the results. Isn't that the point?"

Nakka shook his head, a faint smile touching his lips. "No, Alok. That is where we misunderstand. The software provides calculations, yes, but only you can interpret them, test them, challenge them. You are the engineer, not the software. If you follow blindly, then who is in control?"

Alok sat back, realization dawning in his eyes. "I suppose I've been relying on it too much. But sometimes, it feels like the software knows better."

"The software knows what we tell it," Nakka said, his voice firm. "But it cannot think, it cannot doubt, and it cannot question. That is your role. Mastery is not about using the tool—it is about knowing when the tool's output aligns with reality. That judgment, Alok, is yours alone."

The Journey to Mastery: Training Beyond Mechanics

Nakka knew that using technology effectively required more than knowledge of the software; it required a depth of understanding that came from training, from patience, from questioning. He organized workshops, but these were not the usual tutorials. They were sessions focused on mastery, on the human skill required to make technology meaningful. He encouraged engineers to question outputs, to test calculations, to develop an instinct for when the software's results required scrutiny.

Steps Toward Mastery of Technology:

1. **Advanced Training Sessions on Interpretation**
2. Nakka arranged training that went beyond software mechanics. Engineers learned not only how to operate the programs but how to interpret the data critically, to question results and understand the calculations at a fundamental level.
3. **Case Studies of Real-World Application**

4. He introduced case studies from the engineering field where software errors had led to real-world failures, teaching the engineers that blind trust in outputs could be dangerous. These cases grounded the importance of mastery, turning theory into tangible understanding.

5. **Peer Mentorship and Knowledge Sharing**

6. To cultivate mastery, Nakka paired seasoned engineers with younger ones, encouraging mentorship. He wanted each engineer to understand that mastery was shared knowledge, that experience and insight were as valuable as any software manual.

A Dialogue on Purpose with Saira from Operations

In the midst of these changes, Nakka met with Saira, who managed the operations side of engineering. She had expressed concerns about the reliance on technology, questioning whether the engineers could truly operate without it.

"Saira, do you think technology defines us?" Nakka asked, looking at her intently.

She hesitated, choosing her words carefully. "In some ways, yes. It enhances what we do. Without it, we would be limited. But I also see that, sometimes, we lose sight of our own skills, relying too much on the programs."

"Exactly," Nakka replied. "Technology is our tool, but it must serve us, not enslave us. When we forget our own skills, our own understanding, we lose the very thing that makes us engineers. We become operators, not creators."

Saira nodded, a new understanding lighting her eyes. "So, the goal is balance. To use the technology but not let it control us."

"Balance, yes," Nakka said thoughtfully. "But more than that—purpose. We use technology to amplify our skills, to enhance our ability to create, to solve, to build. But technology without human judgment, without insight, is hollow. Our purpose is to elevate our work, not surrender it to a machine."

Implementing Peer Reviews and Accountability in Software Usage

Nakka introduced a peer review process, where engineers would review each other's software outputs, not just to check for errors but to discuss insights, to share perspectives on interpretation. He believed that by grounding software usage in collaborative review, he could cultivate a culture where technology became a shared journey toward mastery, not a solitary reliance.

Approaches to Integrate Accountability in Technology Use:

1. **Peer Review and Cross-Checking Outputs**
2. Engineers were encouraged to review each other's outputs, fostering a culture of accountability. These reviews were collaborative, discussions on insights rather than mere checks for accuracy.
3. **Refining Judgment Through Real-Time Simulation Testing**
4. Nakka introduced simulation tests, where engineers would validate software outputs through controlled testing. It reinforced the understanding that outputs needed verification, that judgment was an essential layer over technology.
5. **Encouraging Self-Reflection on Results**
6. He asked each engineer to include a brief self-reflection with their outputs—why they trusted a result, where they had doubts, and how they arrived at their conclusions. This practice cultivated mindfulness in their use of technology, a pause to consider rather than blindly follow.

Philosophical Reflection: Mastery as Responsibility

That evening, as Nakka walked through the now-quiet engineering floor, he reflected on the nature of mastery. He saw the rows of computers, the screens that flickered with data, each one representing potential, possibility. But without human insight, he knew that potential was dormant, a promise unfulfilled.

Mastery is not in the tool, he thought. *It is in the one who wields it, in the hand that guides, in the mind that questions.*

He believed that true mastery required more than skill; it required responsibility, a willingness to question, to challenge, to push beyond the surface. Technology, in its raw form, could not answer; it could only produce. It was human insight that transformed that output into something meaningful, something purposeful.

The Unveiling of Mastery in Technology

In the months that followed, Nakka observed a transformation. Engineers worked with a new awareness, a consciousness that was almost tangible. They discussed outputs openly, questioning each other's interpretations, debating approaches. Technology had become a bridge, a means to an end, but they no longer relied on it unthinkingly.

One day, he overheard an exchange between two engineers as they reviewed a simulation output.

"Do you think this data reflects reality?" one asked, pointing to the screen.

"Not entirely," the other replied, thoughtful. "We should run a secondary check. Trust the tool, yes, but let's confirm it."

Nakka felt a quiet satisfaction. The shift he had envisioned was unfolding. They were not just using technology; they were mastering it, making it an extension of their skill, their judgment. This, he knew, was true progress.

Key Takeaways from Nakka's Approach to Technology

1. **Mastery Over Reliance: Human Insight as the Core of Technology Use**
2. Nakka's philosophy emphasized that technology was a tool, but human judgment was the guiding force. By fostering insight over blind reliance, he created a culture of mastery.
3. **Collaborative Review as a Path to Accountability**
4. Through peer reviews and cross-checks, Nakka cultivated a shared journey of accountability, making technology usage a collaborative, mindful process.
5. **Critical Training and Real-World Application to Foster Skepticism and Precision**

6. Training that focused on interpretation, coupled with real-world case studies, taught engineers the importance of questioning, of bringing skepticism to their work with technology.
7. **Reflection and Self-Assessment to Cultivate Purpose**
8. Nakka's emphasis on self-reflection ensured that engineers paused to consider their trust in outputs, grounding their use of technology in purpose, not passivity.

Legacy of Nakka's Vision for Technology

Years later, the organization thrived not only because of its tools but because of its people. Technology had become a partner, an instrument of purpose, its value amplified by the insight and judgment of those who wielded it. Nakka's legacy was not software proficiency; it was mastery—a mastery that turned technology into a true extension of human skill, of purpose, of responsibility.

Nakka had shown them that tools alone do not build mastery. It was the mind, the hand, the insight that made technology valuable. And through that, he had forged an organization where technology was not the master but the servant, a means to purpose, a bridge to progress.

Chapter 6

MEASURING WHAT MATTERS – DATA-DRIVEN DECISION-MAKING

Nakka's Principle: Data as a Guide, Not an Overlord

Nakka observed the numbers on the dashboard screen—the endless scroll of figures and graphs, each one capturing a different element of the organization's progress. But beneath the surface, he saw a problem: the numbers were drowning the organization. Every department, every manager, every employee seemed trapped in a maze of metrics, their actions dictated by a torrent of data that offered more confusion than clarity.

To Nakka, data was essential, yet he viewed it differently. He believed in the power of numbers, but he distrusted their dominance. Data should not be an unyielding ruler but a compass—a guide that pointed the way rather than dictated every step.

Data can reveal truths, he thought. *But without insight, it's nothing more than noise.*

A Dialogue on Data with Priya, Head of Analytics

Nakka sat across from Priya, the head of Analytics, a woman whose dedication to precision was both her strength and her trap. She was meticulous, committed to accuracy, yet she often lost herself in the intricacies of data, her decisions burdened by the need for absolute certainty.

"Priya," he began, "what do you see when you look at these numbers?"

Priya hesitated, then spoke with a hint of pride. "I see patterns, trends. I see the organization's performance captured in numbers. It's... clarity."

Nakka looked at her, his gaze steady. "Clarity? Or just complexity dressed as truth?"

Priya frowned, unsure. "What do you mean?"

"Data is a reflection, Priya," he said, his voice low but intense. "But it is not the truth itself. When we begin to worship numbers as if they are absolute, we lose sight of what they represent. We're not here to serve data. Data should serve us, to show us paths—not to become the path."

Priya listened, her expression one of dawning realization. She had always seen data as an end, the ultimate answer. But Nakka was challenging that belief, suggesting that data was only valuable when it aligned with the organization's purpose, when it pointed toward a meaningful goal.

Redefining Metrics: Choosing What Matters

Nakka knew that the organization needed fewer metrics, not more. He saw the team tracking hundreds of data points, each one a piece of the larger puzzle, yet the pieces never connected. It was information for information's sake, a maze of complexity that obstructed true understanding. He decided to strip down the metrics, focusing only on those that served the organization's purpose.

Steps to Refine Data Metrics:

1. **Identifying Core Metrics Aligned with Vision**
2. Nakka gathered department heads and asked them to define what truly mattered in their roles. The results were surprising; many realized that their metrics were disconnected from the organization's core goals. Together, they distilled the list down to key performance indicators that reflected true impact.
3. **Eliminating Redundant Data Points**
4. He instructed teams to remove any metric that didn't serve a direct purpose. This wasn't about less data; it was about meaningful data. Every metric that remained had to justify its existence, to show how it contributed to the larger mission.

5. **Real-Time Dashboards for Transparency and Action**
6. Nakka introduced real-time dashboards that displayed the core metrics, accessible to all teams. The simplicity of the dashboards became a powerful tool, creating a focus that allowed them to act with purpose rather than react to noise.

A Philosophical Exchange with Rishi on the Value of Intuition

Rishi, the head of Sales, had a habit of disregarding data altogether. To him, intuition mattered more, a personal compass that often clashed with Analytics. Nakka invited him to discuss this tension, knowing that his skepticism held valuable insight.

"Rishi," Nakka began, "why do you dismiss the data?"

Rishi leaned back, his gaze defiant. "Data doesn't understand the ground reality. Numbers don't capture people's instincts, their emotions. I trust what I see, what I feel—not what I'm told by a screen."

"And you're right," Nakka replied, surprising him. "Data alone is hollow. It's a guide, but it doesn't replace insight. Your intuition—if it's aligned with our purpose—is as valuable as any metric. But remember, intuition without grounding can lead to chaos, just as data without vision leads to blindness."

Rishi stared at him, the fire in his eyes dimming to a thoughtful glow. Nakka's words had given him a framework, a way to see his instincts not as rebellion but as complementary to data. He understood now: intuition and data were not enemies but allies, each one anchoring the other.

Establishing Data-Driven Culture without Data Dependency

Nakka sought to cultivate a culture that embraced data without becoming enslaved to it. He introduced data-review meetings where teams discussed the implications of metrics, not just the numbers themselves. He encouraged them to view data as a mirror, reflecting reality but never defining it entirely.

Methods to Establish Balanced Data-Driven Decision-Making:

1. **Contextual Interpretation Sessions**
2. Nakka introduced weekly sessions where data was reviewed in the context of real scenarios. Teams discussed what the numbers meant, how they aligned with ongoing projects, and where their insights could improve decision-making.
3. **Encouraging Hypotheses and Testing Assumptions**
4. Rather than taking data at face value, he asked teams to form hypotheses, to test their assumptions against the numbers. This approach fostered critical thinking, a habit of questioning that made data a tool of validation rather than an unquestioned authority.
5. **Cross-Departmental Data Debates**
6. Nakka organized debates where departments could challenge each other's metrics, examining how one department's success might affect another's. These discussions brought an understanding of interdependence, a recognition that metrics were interconnected, just as the organization was.

Philosophical Reflection: Data as Reflection, Not Reality

That evening, as he sat alone, Nakka pondered the nature of data. He saw it as a mirror—reflecting the organization's progress, capturing a moment in time. Yet he understood its limitations, its inability to convey depth, intuition, vision.

Data is like a lighthouse in the distance, he thought. *It can guide us, but we must navigate the waters ourselves. The journey is not defined by the light alone, but by the skill of the sailor.*

He knew that relying solely on data was a risk, a shortcut that sacrificed intuition and understanding. True decision-making came from balance, from the integration of insight and information, where neither was subordinate. He resolved to guide the organization toward this balance, to make data an asset but never an absolute.

The Impact of Focused, Purpose-Driven Metrics

In the months that followed, the organization began to change. Teams reported with clarity, their actions focused on metrics that mattered. The noise had subsided, replaced by a calm that allowed them to make decisions with purpose. Data was no longer an obstacle; it was a guide, a compass pointing toward goals rather than dictating every movement.

One day, he overheard a manager advising a team member:

"Remember, data gives us direction, but it's up to us to find the way."

Nakka felt a quiet pride. They had grasped the essence of his vision, the balance he had fought to instill. Data was now a tool, a servant of purpose rather than a master.

Key Takeaways from Nakka's Approach to Data

1. **Purpose-Driven Metrics to Eliminate Noise**
2. By focusing on essential metrics, Nakka transformed data from an overwhelming force into a clear guide that aligned with the organization's vision.
3. **Intuition and Insight as Complements to Data**
4. Nakka valued human intuition alongside data, creating a culture where insight and metrics worked in harmony, each anchoring the other.
5. **Contextual Interpretation to Foster Critical Thinking**
6. By reviewing data in context, Nakka taught his teams to question, to interpret metrics not as absolutes but as reflections, fostering a culture of critical thinking.
7. **Cross-Departmental Collaboration for Interconnected Metrics**
8. Through debates and discussions, Nakka encouraged departments to understand their interdependence, showing that metrics in one area influenced others, just as in the organization itself.

Legacy of Nakka's Vision for Data-Driven Decision-Making

Years later, the organization had grown, but it retained the clarity and balance Nakka had instilled. Data was an integral part of their process, but it was balanced by insight, by intuition, by purpose. The organization's decisions were not driven by numbers alone but by a deeper understanding of what those numbers represented.

Nakka's legacy was one of balance, a vision that data and insight together could create clarity, that metrics could be a guide but never a replacement for human understanding. He had shown them that true wisdom lay not in numbers but in the mind that interpreted them, the vision that brought them meaning.

Chapter 7

THE POWER OF SIMPLICITY – CHECKLISTS

Nakka's Insight: Complexity is a Mask; Simplicity is Strength

Nakka believed in the art of simplicity, yet he recognized the subtle irony: simplicity was not always simple. As the organization grew, he saw chaos taking root, with small errors compounding into larger issues. Overlooked tasks, forgotten details, missed steps—all these "minor" oversights threatened to unravel even the most meticulously crafted plans.

To Nakka, this wasn't merely an issue of logistics. He saw it as a failure of clarity, an erosion of purpose. If each step, each task, each decision could not be executed with precision, then the entire operation was compromised. He knew that the answer lay not in complexity but in simplicity—a simplicity that was so often misunderstood and undervalued.

True simplicity is a discipline, he thought. *It demands clarity, precision, and, above all, respect for detail.*

A Conversation on Complexity with Meera, Head of Quality Assurance

Nakka sought out Meera, the head of Quality Assurance, to discuss the issue. She had been overwhelmed by a string of project delays, her team constantly rechecking details that had been missed earlier in the process.

"Meera," he asked, his tone thoughtful, "why do you think these mistakes keep happening?"

She sighed, frustration evident. "Everyone is rushing, Nakka. There's no time to go back and check each detail, so things slip through. We're drowning in tasks, trying to manage it all without a clear process."

Nakka nodded, his gaze intense. "Exactly. We're fighting complexity with complexity. We think more steps, more checks, more layers will create order. But complexity is not strength—it is a mask that hides inefficiency. What we need, Meera, is simplicity. A method that guides, that doesn't allow room for error."

Meera looked at him, intrigued. "You're suggesting… checklists? Isn't that too basic?"

"Basic?" Nakka replied, his voice firm. "No, Meera. Checklists are not basic; they are fundamental. When we simplify, we create clarity, focus. A checklist is more than a list—it is a promise to honor each step, to respect each detail. Simplicity is not the absence of complexity. It is the mastery of it."

Building Discipline Through Checklists

Determined to prove the power of simplicity, Nakka introduced checklists for every critical process. But these were no ordinary checklists. They were tools of discipline, of respect for detail. Each checklist was crafted with care, each item a vital component, ensuring that no step was overlooked, no task forgotten.

Steps to Implement Effective Checklists:

1. **Identifying Essential Tasks and Their Sequence**
2. Nakka worked with teams to define the most critical tasks in each process. He insisted on clarity, on understanding the purpose behind each step. Every item on the checklist had to contribute to the mission, to the purpose of the project.
3. **Creating Checkpoints, Not Just Steps**
4. These checklists included checkpoints—moments of reflection where team members could pause, review, and ensure precision before moving forward. It wasn't just about ticking off tasks; it was about honoring each one.

5. **Establishing Ownership and Accountability**
6. Nakka made it clear that each person using a checklist was responsible for the integrity of their work. A checked box was not a formality; it was a signature, a mark of accountability that each step had been completed with intention and care.

A Philosophical Exchange with Saira on the Nature of Precision

Nakka met with Saira once again, knowing her to be a leader who understood the value of precision. She, too, had seen the rise of chaos in the organization and had been searching for ways to bring order without stifling creativity.

"Saira," Nakka began, "do you believe precision can coexist with creativity?"

Saira thought for a moment. "I used to think creativity was free-form, unrestricted. But now I see that without structure, creativity becomes chaos. Precision, I think, can be the foundation of true creativity."

Nakka nodded, a spark of satisfaction in his eyes. "Exactly. Precision is not the enemy of creativity; it is its ally. When we use checklists, we free the mind to focus on the essential, on what truly matters. Creativity thrives not in chaos but in the clarity of purpose."

"So, checklists don't limit us. They allow us to focus," Saira concluded, her expression one of quiet conviction.

"Precisely," Nakka said, his tone resolute. "Simplicity is strength because it directs focus. Each task, each step, becomes an act of purpose. When we honor simplicity, we find power—not in the complexity we add, but in the clarity we preserve."

Reinforcing the Culture of Simplicity and Precision

Nakka understood that simplicity had to be nurtured, reinforced. He encouraged a culture where checklists were seen not as burdens but as tools of mastery. He introduced checklist audits, where teams would review each item, refining, removing anything that did not serve a purpose. It was an exercise in discipline, a ritual that honored the value of precision.

Methods to Strengthen Checklist Culture:

1. **Checklist Audits for Continuous Improvement**
2. Nakka implemented monthly audits where teams would assess each checklist, asking if every item was necessary, if it served the project's purpose. This refinement process kept checklists relevant and purposeful.
3. **Celebrating Precision and Attention to Detail**
4. He began to recognize team members who demonstrated exceptional discipline, who completed checklists not out of obligation but as an act of respect for their craft. This celebration of precision elevated simplicity to a virtue, a point of pride.
5. **Encouraging Reflection After Completion**
6. At the end of each project, Nakka encouraged teams to reflect on the checklist process, discussing what worked, what could be improved. It wasn't just about finishing; it was about learning, evolving, mastering the art of simplicity.

Philosophical Reflection: Simplicity as Respect

Alone in his office, Nakka reflected on the essence of simplicity. To him, simplicity was more than efficiency. It was respect—respect for each task, each step, each detail. Complexity was often a mask, a way to hide indecision or lack of clarity. But simplicity stripped away the unnecessary, leaving only what was essential, what was true.

Simplicity is honesty, he thought. *It is the courage to eliminate the excess, to focus on what truly matters. In simplicity, we find strength, we find purpose.*

He knew that each checklist represented a commitment, a promise that the work would be done with integrity. There was power in this ritual, in the act of honoring each detail. He believed that simplicity was the foundation of mastery, that through simplicity, they could achieve excellence.

The Impact of Checklists on Precision and Performance

In the following months, Nakka observed a transformation. Projects ran more smoothly, errors decreased, and deadlines were met with consistency. The organization had found a rhythm, a harmony in simplicity that allowed them to focus on what mattered most. The checklists were no longer seen as mundane but as tools of discipline, symbols of precision.

One day, he overheard a project manager explaining the purpose of checklists to a new employee:

"These aren't just steps. They're reminders of our commitment to quality, to excellence. Each item we check off is a promise kept."

Nakka felt a deep sense of fulfillment. His vision had taken root. The organization understood now that simplicity was not a shortcut; it was an expression of respect, of dedication to purpose.

Key Takeaways from Nakka's Approach to Simplicity

1. **Simplicity as Precision, Not Limitation**
2. Nakka's philosophy turned checklists into tools of mastery, showing that simplicity wasn't about limiting creativity but about directing focus and precision.
3. **Checklists as Acts of Accountability and Ownership**
4. Each checklist item represented a commitment. By assigning ownership, Nakka fostered a culture where completion was a mark of integrity, not mere formality.
5. **Continuous Improvement Through Reflection**
6. The monthly checklist audits and reflections reinforced a culture of learning, where each process was refined, each step honored, creating an environment of continuous improvement.
7. **Respect for Detail as a Foundation for Excellence**
8. Through checklists, Nakka instilled a respect for detail, a recognition that true strength lay not in complexity but in the disciplined pursuit of simplicity.

Legacy of Nakka's Vision for Simplicity

In the years that followed, the organization thrived. Projects moved with precision, each step a reflection of commitment, of purpose. Nakka's legacy was not just a process; it was a belief—that simplicity, when honored, could lead to mastery, that discipline in the smallest details could build a foundation for greatness.

Nakka had shown them that simplicity was strength, that respect for detail was the pathway to excellence. Through checklists, he had given them a tool not just for efficiency but for purpose—a purpose that would define their work, their values, and their legacy.

Chapter 8

CUSTOMER-CENTRIC THINKING – ALIGNING WITH CUSTOMER NEEDS

Nakka's Belief: Success Lies in Understanding, Not Just Selling

As Nakka walked through the bustling corridors of his company, he felt the pulse of activity. Sales pitches were being crafted, marketing campaigns brainstormed, products refined. Yet, he sensed something essential was slipping away—a connection to the very people they were serving. The customer, he realized, had become an abstract concept, a distant goal rather than a presence that guided their every action.

To Nakka, this was not merely an oversight but a profound disconnection. He believed that to truly serve, they needed to understand the customer as more than a data point, more than a sales target. The customer was a partner, a presence that shaped the company's purpose.

We do not merely sell to customers, he thought. *We are here because of them. Understanding is not a step toward success—it is the foundation of it.*

A Conversation with the Marketing Team on Customer Focus

Nakka gathered the marketing team, sensing that their efforts, though sincere, lacked the clarity of true connection. They spoke of demographics, conversion rates, trends, yet he saw that they were missing something vital—the human aspect.

"Tell me," Nakka asked, his tone measured, "who is our customer?"

The team exchanged glances, reciting the familiar data. "We target mid-sized companies, decision-makers in tech industries, primarily in the 30-50 age range..."

Nakka shook his head gently, a hint of disappointment in his gaze. "No, I am not asking for statistics. I am asking, who is our customer? What do they need? What do they fear? What is it they truly want?"

A silence fell over the team. They had been focused on selling, on reaching targets. But now Nakka was asking them to understand the customer's reality, to see the world through their eyes.

"If we cannot feel our customer's pain, if we cannot see their vision," Nakka continued, his voice soft but resolute, "we are simply selling products. But if we understand, truly understand, then we are building something greater. We are creating solutions, forging connections, serving a purpose beyond profit."

The team listened, a new awareness stirring within them. Nakka's words had redefined the customer as a partner, a collaborator in their shared journey.

Building Empathy for the Customer: Strategies and Actions

Nakka knew that empathy couldn't be manufactured; it had to be cultivated, nurtured. He implemented initiatives that brought the customer's perspective into every department, ensuring that they saw the customer not as an end but as a companion in their journey.

Steps to Foster Customer-Centric Thinking:

1. **Direct Customer Interaction for All Teams**
2. Nakka insisted that each department engage directly with customers, even if indirectly related to sales or support. Engineers spoke with end-users, marketers attended client feedback sessions, and finance managers reviewed customer stories. It was immersion, an experience designed to build genuine empathy.

3. **Customer Personas with Depth and Insight**
4. He tasked teams with creating detailed customer personas—not just profiles but stories. These personas included the customer's goals, struggles, fears, and dreams. They were living documents, evolving with each interaction, capturing the human essence behind the metrics.
5. **Customer Champions in Every Department**
6. Nakka appointed "Customer Champions" within each team, individuals responsible for representing the customer's voice in all discussions. These champions were advocates, ensuring that every decision, every strategy, aligned with the customer's needs and values.

A Philosophical Exchange with Alok, Head of Product Development

Nakka met with Alok, the head of Product Development, whose focus on innovation was unmatched. Yet Nakka sensed that Alok, though brilliant, sometimes innovated for innovation's sake, disconnected from the real needs of the customer.

"Alok," Nakka asked, his voice contemplative, "why do we build?"

Alok looked at him, slightly puzzled. "To create better products, to stay ahead in the market."

"But for whom?" Nakka pressed, his gaze unwavering. "Do we build for the sake of novelty, or do we build to solve a problem, to meet a need?"

Alok paused, considering. "I suppose… we build for the customer. But sometimes, the market demands innovation, and we follow."

"The market demands, yes," Nakka replied, his voice carrying a quiet conviction. "But the customer's need—this is not a demand. It is a truth, a reality we must understand. If we build only to compete, we lose sight of purpose. But if we build to serve, to fulfill, then every innovation, every product, carries meaning."

Alok listened, understanding now that innovation was not just progress but purpose. He saw that true creation was not in the features but in the solutions, in the impact each product could have on the lives of their customers.

Embedding Customer-Centric Values in Every Action

Nakka took concrete steps to ensure that customer-centricity became part of the organizational fabric. He introduced "Customer Focus" sessions where teams reviewed feedback, not as criticism but as insights to guide their next steps. The sessions were structured around understanding, not metrics—stories over statistics, empathy over efficiency.

Methods to Embed Customer Focus in the Organization:

1. **Monthly Customer Feedback Forums**
2. Every month, Nakka held forums where teams discussed recent customer feedback. These sessions focused not on problems but on understanding what the feedback revealed about the customer's reality, their experience, and their expectations.
3. **Continuous Persona Updates and Real-Time Customer Insights**
4. He encouraged teams to update customer personas regularly, ensuring they stayed relevant. Real-time insights were shared across departments, a continuous reminder that the customer's reality was ever-changing, and they must adapt with it.
5. **Customer Appreciation Rituals to Celebrate Connection**
6. Nakka believed in celebrating customers, not only for their loyalty but as partners. He introduced rituals where teams acknowledged milestones with customers, personalized gestures that went beyond transactions, affirming the connection they were building.

Philosophical Reflection: The Customer as Partner, Not Target

As he sat alone one evening, Nakka reflected on the essence of customer-centric thinking. He saw the customer not as a goal but as a reason, a purpose that validated their efforts. To him, the customer was not the end but the beginning—the origin of every idea, every innovation, every effort.

To serve is to understand, he thought. *And to understand, we must see the customer not as a target, but as a partner in our journey. Success lies not in what we sell, but in what we fulfill.*

He believed that true success was not in transactions but in transformations—in changing the lives of those they served, in meeting needs that ran deeper than products or services. In this belief, he found purpose, a reason that guided his vision and shaped his every decision.

The Transformation of Customer Relations

Months later, Nakka observed a change. Teams spoke of customers with a new sense of respect, of partnership. They no longer saw customers as distant figures but as allies, as individuals whose lives they could impact. Product designs became more thoughtful, marketing campaigns more genuine, service more compassionate.

One day, he overheard a marketing executive discussing a campaign.

"This isn't just about what we offer. It's about what they need, about how we can help them achieve it."

Nakka felt a quiet satisfaction. His vision had taken root, a vision where the customer was no longer a number but a reason. They had begun to see that their purpose was not only to sell but to serve.

Key Takeaways from Nakka's Approach to Customer-Centric Thinking

1. **Understanding the Customer Beyond Statistics**
2. By encouraging empathy and direct interaction, Nakka transformed the customer from a target into a partner, fostering a culture where needs took precedence over numbers.
3. **Continuous Adaptation to Changing Customer Realities**
4. The evolving customer personas and monthly feedback forums kept the organization in tune with the customer's reality, ensuring that their strategies were always relevant.

5. **Customer-Centric Innovation as Purposeful Progress**
6. Nakka's conversations with leaders like Alok redefined innovation as a service to the customer, where progress was guided by purpose, not merely market demand.
7. **Celebrating the Customer as a Partner, Not a Transaction**
8. Through customer appreciation rituals and personalized connections, Nakka reinforced the idea that every customer was a partner, a relationship that transcended mere sales.

Legacy of Nakka's Vision for Customer-Centricity

In the years that followed, the organization flourished, not because of its products but because of its purpose. Customers were loyal, not merely satisfied but genuinely connected, finding in the company a partner that understood and respected their needs. Nakka's legacy was not only a customer-focused culture but a belief—that to serve was to understand, and that true success lay not in sales but in significance.

Nakka had shown them that the customer was more than a goal—they were the reason. Through this belief, he had built a foundation that placed understanding at the core, a purpose that gave life to every product, every service, every interaction.

Chapter 9

INNOVATION AND CREATIVITY – FOSTERING A CULTURE OF INNOVATION

Nakka's Belief: True Innovation Demands Freedom from Fear

The hum of progress filled the company halls, each department striving to create, to improve, to innovate. Yet, Nakka sensed a subtle inhibition, a reluctance that crept into even the most promising ideas. Innovation was stifled by hesitation, creativity dulled by the quiet but pervasive fear of failure.

To Nakka, this hesitation was a profound barrier to true progress. He believed that creativity could not flourish where fear was present. Innovation required freedom—freedom to experiment, to fail, to try again. He saw that their efforts were bound by invisible chains, a collective caution that hindered the potential for genuine breakthroughs.

Innovation is not about perfection, he thought. *It is about courage, the courage to leap into the unknown, to build without fear of falling.*

A Conversation on Risk with the Executive Team

Nakka gathered the executive team, sensing that they too had begun to lean towards safe decisions, proven paths. As they discussed upcoming projects, he could hear the caution in their voices, the insistence on guarantees, on minimizing risk. But to Nakka, risk was not an enemy—it was a catalyst, a force that spurred growth.

"Why do you think we fear risk?" he asked, his tone reflective.

The executives exchanged glances, some defensive, others resigned. "It's because failure has a cost," one of them said. "We can't afford mistakes."

Nakka's gaze was calm, penetrating. "And what is the cost of refusing to take risks? What do we lose when we fear failure more than we value progress?"

A silence followed. They were accustomed to caution, to predictability. But Nakka's words challenged this security, asked them to question if they had become protectors of the present rather than builders of the future.

"I am not asking for recklessness," he continued, "but for courage. True innovation requires that we move beyond safety. We must not ask, 'Will this succeed?' but 'Is this worth the risk?' Because only when we risk for purpose can we build something meaningful."

The executives sat in thoughtful silence. Nakka had given them a new perspective, a way to see risk not as a cost but as an investment, a step toward something greater than the status quo.

Creating a Space for Innovation: Building the Lab of Freedom

Determined to dismantle the fear of failure, Nakka established an innovation lab—a space dedicated to experimentation, to boundless creativity. But this was more than a lab; it was a sanctuary for ideas, a place where employees were free to explore, to create without constraints. He wanted them to know that here, failure was not a setback but a stepping stone.

Steps to Foster a Culture of Innovation:

1. **Creating Freedom Zones for Risk-Taking**
2. In the lab, Nakka removed the traditional rules, establishing "freedom zones" where employees could experiment without the fear of immediate consequences. This space was sacred, a reminder that creativity needed room to breathe.

3. **Celebrating Failures as Lessons, Not Losses**
4. He introduced the concept of "Learning Failures"—projects that didn't succeed but taught valuable lessons. Each failure was analyzed, celebrated for its insights. This reframed failure as growth, transforming fear into curiosity.
5. **Innovation Champions to Foster and Protect Ideas**
6. Nakka appointed Innovation Champions within each department, individuals whose sole purpose was to nurture and protect ideas, to push boundaries and encourage others to take calculated risks. These champions became guardians of creativity, advocates of bold thinking.

A Philosophical Exchange on Progress with Shalini, Head of Research

Nakka sought out Shalini, the head of Research, a scientist whose dedication to precision was often at odds with the unpredictability of innovation. She valued certainty, accuracy, and he knew that her approach was both a strength and a limitation.

"Shalini," he asked, his tone gentle, "what do you believe progress truly is?"

She thought for a moment. "Progress is improvement, a way to make things better."

"And do you think progress is always predictable? That it can be measured, controlled?"

Shalini looked at him, understanding his point. "I suppose not. But uncertainty… it undermines reliability."

"Yes, it does," Nakka agreed. "But uncertainty is also where breakthroughs lie. When we control too tightly, we limit our vision. Real progress is not in doing what is certain, but in exploring what is possible. True innovation is not predictable; it is transformative."

Shalini nodded, her perspective shifting. She realized that her drive for certainty had, in some ways, confined her. She understood now that innovation wasn't just an improvement of what was known but a journey into what could be.

Embedding Innovation in Everyday Actions

Nakka took steps to ensure that innovation became part of the organization's daily life, not just an occasional venture. He introduced "idea sessions" where teams could discuss new concepts openly, without restriction. He encouraged them to question norms, to challenge assumptions, to see the familiar through new eyes.

Methods to Embed Innovation as a Core Value:

1. **Weekly Open Idea Sessions for Cross-Department Collaboration**
2. Nakka introduced open sessions where departments shared ideas without judgment, fostering a culture of cross-departmental creativity. It was a meeting of minds, a gathering of perspectives that broke down silos.
3. **Fail-Fast, Learn-Fast Approach to Rapid Experimentation**
4. He encouraged a "fail-fast, learn-fast" mentality, allowing teams to experiment rapidly, learn, and pivot as needed. This approach removed the stigma from failure, framing it as an essential part of growth.
5. **Annual Innovation Awards for Courageous Thinking**
6. To honor the spirit of creativity, Nakka established annual innovation awards, celebrating those who took bold risks, who ventured beyond certainty. These awards recognized not just success but the courage to pursue the unknown.

Philosophical Reflection: Innovation as Purposeful Creation

As he sat alone in the quiet of his office, Nakka reflected on the nature of innovation. He saw it as more than mere advancement; it was a form of creation, an expression of purpose. To him, innovation was not about being first or best but about adding value, creating something meaningful, something that would endure.

Innovation is the courage to dream, to build beyond what is seen, he thought. *It is the bridge between the present and the possible, a journey that requires courage and conviction.*

He believed that true innovation required not just skill but vision, a willingness to see beyond the immediate, to take risks not for profit but for purpose. In this belief, he found clarity—a clarity that allowed him to guide the organization toward a future shaped not by fear but by bold, purposeful action.

The Transformation of Creativity and Risk-Taking

Over time, Nakka observed a transformation. The organization's approach to risk had changed, caution replaced by a quiet but steady courage. Teams were unafraid to experiment, to try, to fail, and to try again. The innovation lab became a place of discovery, where new ideas thrived, where each failure was a lesson, each success a testament to courage.

One day, he overheard a young engineer explaining her approach to a new project.

"I don't know if this will work," she said, her tone calm, resolute. "But it's worth the risk. If it doesn't succeed, I'll learn something valuable for the next attempt."

Nakka felt a deep satisfaction. His vision had taken root. They had begun to see that innovation was not about certainty but about courage, about creating value beyond the known, beyond the predictable.

Key Takeaways from Nakka's Approach to Innovation

1. **Risk as a Catalyst for Purposeful Progress**
2. Nakka's belief in the value of risk transformed caution into courage, showing that true innovation required stepping beyond the boundaries of certainty.
3. **Failure as a Tool for Growth, Not a Measure of Loss**
4. By celebrating learning failures, he reframed mistakes as stepping stones, nurturing a culture where each setback was an opportunity for growth.
5. **Cross-Departmental Collaboration to Break Down Silos**
6. Through open idea sessions and Innovation Champions, Nakka fostered a culture of shared creativity, where each department became part of a unified journey toward progress.

7. **Honoring Courageous Thinking as the Heart of Innovation**
8. The annual awards celebrated not only success but the bravery to pursue the unknown, establishing innovation as an expression of purpose, of vision.

Legacy of Nakka's Vision for Innovation

In the years that followed, the organization became known not for its products alone but for its courage, its willingness to take risks, to innovate with purpose. Employees felt empowered, not bound by fear but driven by curiosity, by the desire to create something meaningful.

Nakka's legacy was not merely a culture of innovation but a belief—that progress was not a straight line but a journey shaped by courage, by conviction. He had shown them that true creativity lay not in perfection but in purpose, that the path to greatness was not paved with certainty but with the courage to build beyond it.

Chapter 10

DIVERSITY AND INCLUSION – BUILDING A COLLABORATIVE, INCLUSIVE CULTURE

Nakka's Belief: Strength Lies in Embracing Differences

Walking through the company corridors, Nakka observed the diversity around him—different backgrounds, voices, perspectives. Yet, he sensed an invisible barrier, an undercurrent that kept this diversity from becoming true unity. People worked together, yes, but they worked within their silos, each team, each culture, each voice guarded, contained.

To Nakka, this separation was not merely a missed opportunity but a fundamental weakness. He believed that true strength came from embracing differences, from building a culture where every perspective, every voice, was not only welcomed but valued. Diversity, he thought, was not a demographic—it was an approach, a way of seeing the world through a multifaceted lens.

Inclusion is not about blending into sameness, he reflected. *It is about amplifying each unique voice, creating a harmony that strengthens us all.*

A Conversation on Unity with Ravi, Head of Human Resources

Nakka sat with Ravi, the head of HR, a man known for his diplomatic skills, his ability to navigate the complexities of the workplace. They discussed recent team challenges, instances where cultural misunderstandings had led to friction, where the organization's diversity felt more like a barrier than a strength.

"Ravi," Nakka asked, his tone calm but probing, "do you think we understand what inclusion truly means?"

Ravi hesitated, choosing his words carefully. "I think we try to be inclusive, but sometimes… it feels like we're just tolerating differences rather than embracing them."

Nakka nodded, a hint of sadness in his eyes. "Tolerance is not enough, Ravi. Tolerance suggests a distance, a separation. Inclusion, true inclusion, means more. It means seeing each difference as a contribution, a strength. It means finding the unity within diversity, the connection that binds us all."

Ravi listened, understanding that Nakka was challenging him to go beyond surface-level inclusion, to create a culture where diversity wasn't a formality but a value, a strength that everyone recognized and celebrated.

Building an Inclusive Culture: Actions and Commitments

Determined to transform diversity into unity, Nakka introduced initiatives to break down silos, to bring teams together in ways that honored each individual's perspective. He knew that inclusion could not be mandated; it had to be nurtured, woven into the fabric of daily interactions.

Steps to Foster Diversity and Inclusion:

1. **Inclusive Hiring Practices Focused on Perspective**
2. Nakka worked with HR to redefine hiring practices, focusing on diversity not just as a checklist but as a source of perspective. They sought individuals whose experiences, backgrounds, and ideas would broaden the organization's vision, bringing new insights and approaches.
3. **Cultural Awareness and Sensitivity Training**
4. He introduced training sessions that went beyond compliance, focusing on empathy, understanding, and respect. These sessions encouraged employees to see each other not as different but as individuals with unique strengths, creating bonds that transcended backgrounds.

5. **Cross-Cultural Project Teams to Foster Collaboration**
6. Nakka established cross-cultural teams for major projects, intentionally blending backgrounds and experiences. These teams were more than collaborations; they were exercises in unity, spaces where each voice contributed to a shared goal.

A Philosophical Exchange on Difference with Aisha, Head of Operations

Nakka met with Aisha, the head of Operations, whose background was different from most of her colleagues. She often struggled to balance her identity with the demands of her role, feeling the pressure to conform to a single, uniform standard.

"Aisha," he asked, his voice gentle but unwavering, "do you feel valued for who you are, or for what you conform to?"

Aisha looked at him, the weight of the question evident in her eyes. "I suppose… sometimes it feels like I'm valued for fitting in, for blending with the others."

"But that is not true value," Nakka replied, his tone intense. "True value is found in authenticity, in honoring each person's identity. We do not grow by blending into sameness, Aisha. We grow by celebrating each unique perspective, each voice that brings something irreplaceable to our work."

Aisha listened, understanding now that her differences were not something to hide but to share, to contribute. She felt a newfound confidence, a recognition that her voice, her identity, was an asset, a strength.

Nurturing Unity Through Individual Empowerment

Nakka took deliberate steps to embed inclusion within the organization, not as an initiative but as a core value. He created spaces for open dialogue, for conversations that went beyond work, spaces where individuals could share their stories, their experiences, their perspectives.

Methods to Embed Inclusion in Daily Practice:

1. **Story Circles to Share Personal Journeys**
2. Nakka introduced "Story Circles," sessions where employees shared personal stories, their journeys, their perspectives. These circles became powerful experiences, breaking down barriers, building empathy, and transforming differences into connections.
3. **Mentorship Programs Across Departments and Backgrounds**
4. He established mentorship programs that paired individuals from different backgrounds, fostering relationships that transcended work. These mentorships created bonds, building understanding and trust that strengthened the fabric of the organization.
5. **Celebrating Cultural Milestones and Traditions**
6. Nakka encouraged teams to celebrate cultural milestones, creating an environment that recognized and valued each person's heritage. These celebrations became moments of unity, of shared joy, where diversity was celebrated openly, proudly.

Philosophical Reflection: Diversity as Collective Strength

In the quiet of his office, Nakka reflected on the nature of diversity, of inclusion. To him, diversity was more than demographics; it was a tapestry, a complex blend of experiences, perspectives, strengths. He believed that inclusion was not merely about acceptance but about integration, about weaving each unique thread into a stronger whole.

Strength lies not in uniformity but in unity, he thought. *Inclusion is not a goal but a journey, a commitment to see each person, each difference, as a part of the whole.*

He knew that in a world that often valued sameness, true inclusion was a radical act, an affirmation that each individual's voice mattered. And in this belief, he found purpose—a purpose that guided his vision for the organization, a purpose that made diversity a strength, a foundation for resilience.

The Transformation Toward Inclusion and Unity

Months later, Nakka observed a change. Teams worked with a new sense of respect, of understanding. The Story Circles had created bonds, the mentorships had fostered trust, the cultural celebrations had built pride. Diversity was no longer a formality but a strength, a shared value that united them all.

One day, he overheard a team member sharing her experience in a Story Circle.

"I felt heard, valued. I'm not just an employee here. I'm a part of something bigger."

Nakka felt a quiet satisfaction. His vision had taken root. The organization was no longer a collection of individuals but a unified whole, a place where each person's identity, perspective, and experience contributed to their shared success.

Key Takeaways from Nakka's Approach to Diversity and Inclusion

1. **Diversity as Perspective, Not Demographic**
2. By focusing on perspective in hiring and team-building, Nakka transformed diversity from a statistic into a source of strength, an approach that valued each individual's unique insight.
3. **Inclusion as Empathy and Understanding**
4. Through Story Circles and cultural sensitivity training, he cultivated empathy, creating an environment where differences were not only accepted but valued, where each person felt seen and understood.
5. **Unity Through Cross-Cultural Collaboration**
6. The cross-cultural project teams and mentorship programs built bridges, turning diversity into unity, creating connections that strengthened the organization as a whole.
7. **Celebration of Identity as a Source of Pride**
8. By encouraging the celebration of cultural milestones, Nakka made inclusion a visible, shared value, creating a sense of pride and belonging that resonated throughout the organization.

Legacy of Nakka's Vision for Inclusion

In the years that followed, the organization thrived, not only because of its goals but because of its people. Employees felt a deep connection, a sense of belonging that went beyond work. They were not just a team; they were a community, a collective strengthened by the diversity within it.

Nakka's legacy was not simply an inclusive culture but a belief—that strength lay in unity, that diversity was not a barrier but a bridge, a foundation for resilience. He had shown them that true inclusion was not just about welcoming differences but about valuing them, integrating them, building a future that honored each voice, each perspective.

Through his vision, Nakka had woven diversity into the fabric of the organization, creating a culture where inclusion was not only a value but a strength, a testament to the power of unity in diversity.

Chapter 11

BUILDING A RESILIENT CULTURE – VALUES THAT ENDURE

Nakka's Conviction: A Culture Without Values Is an Empire Without a Foundation

Nakka observed the organization's rapid growth with pride, yet he felt a quiet unease. As new employees joined, as departments expanded, he sensed that something essential was slipping away. The values that had once defined the organization—integrity, dedication, respect—seemed to fade beneath the pressures of growth, the demands of productivity. He saw that the company was at a crossroads, that without a strong foundation of values, they risked becoming hollow, driven only by profit, devoid of purpose.

To Nakka, culture was more than an atmosphere. It was a foundation, the bedrock on which every action, every decision, was built. Without values, they were vulnerable, an empire built on sand. He knew that if they were to endure, they needed to remember who they were, what they stood for.

Culture is not what we say we believe—it is what we do every day, he thought. *Values are not words; they are actions, commitments that must be lived.*

A Discussion on Integrity with Priya, a New Manager

One afternoon, Nakka met with Priya, a young manager who had joined recently. She was ambitious, eager to make her mark, but he sensed a tension within her—a conflict between the drive for results and the commitment to values.

"Priya," Nakka began, his voice steady, "what does integrity mean to you?"

She hesitated, then spoke with uncertainty. "Integrity is… doing what is right, I suppose, even when it's difficult."

"But what is right?" he pressed gently. "Is it achieving results at any cost? Or is it remembering our purpose, our values, even when they challenge us?"

Priya looked at him, realization dawning in her eyes. "So integrity isn't just honesty. It's a commitment to values, a loyalty to something greater than success."

Nakka nodded, a quiet conviction in his gaze. "Exactly, Priya. Integrity means that we do not compromise our values for results. It means that every action, every decision, reflects who we are, what we stand for. Without integrity, success is empty—a victory that leaves us hollow."

Reinforcing Core Values: Actions and Rituals

Determined to root values deeply within the organization, Nakka took steps to make them visible, tangible. He wanted values not as slogans on walls but as actions, rituals that reminded everyone of their shared commitment.

Steps to Foster a Values-Driven Culture:

1. **Values Workshops to Reflect and Reaffirm**
2. Nakka organized workshops where employees from all levels came together to discuss the organization's core values. These sessions weren't lectures but conversations, spaces where each person could reflect, share, and commit to the principles that guided them.
3. **Recognition of Values in Action**
4. He introduced a program that recognized employees who exemplified the organization's values. Each month, peers nominated colleagues who demonstrated integrity, respect, and dedication. It was more than recognition; it was a celebration of character, a reminder that values were not just ideals but lived truths.

5. **Values Ambassadors to Uphold the Culture**
6. Nakka appointed "Values Ambassadors"—individuals within each department responsible for embodying and promoting the organization's values. These ambassadors were guardians of the culture, ensuring that actions aligned with principles, that decisions upheld the organization's identity.

A Philosophical Exchange on Legacy with Ramesh, Head of Operations

Nakka met with Ramesh, the Head of Operations, a man whose focus on efficiency sometimes clashed with the organization's values. Ramesh believed in results, in getting things done, and Nakka saw the conflict between this pragmatism and the values they sought to uphold.

"Ramesh," he asked, his tone thoughtful, "what legacy do you want to leave?"

Ramesh looked at him, surprised by the question. "I suppose… I want to leave a successful operation, something efficient, productive."

"And what do you believe success means?" Nakka pressed. "Is it simply efficiency? Or is it building something that endures, something that stands firm because it is grounded in values?"

Ramesh considered his words, understanding now that success was more than results. "Perhaps… success is not just in what we achieve, but in how we achieve it, in the values that guide us."

"Exactly," Nakka replied, his voice strong. "Our legacy is not measured by profit but by purpose, by the integrity with which we build. Without values, success is fleeting. But with values, we create something enduring, something that reflects who we are, even after we are gone."

Ramesh nodded, seeing now that his actions, his decisions, were not merely tasks but contributions to a legacy, a culture that would outlast them all.

Embedding Values Through Daily Practices

Nakka took concrete steps to weave values into daily practices, creating a culture where each action, each decision, was an expression of their shared identity. He encouraged employees to reflect on the values in their work, to see each task as an opportunity to honor their commitments.

Methods to Reinforce Values in Daily Actions:

1. **Weekly Reflections on Values in Team Meetings**
2. Nakka introduced a ritual where teams reflected on how they had lived the organization's values that week. These reflections became powerful moments of accountability, reminders that values were not optional but essential.
3. **Decision-Making Frameworks Aligned with Core Principles**
4. He developed frameworks for decision-making that aligned with the organization's values, ensuring that every choice, every strategy upheld their principles. This framework became a guide, a standard that reminded them of their purpose.
5. **Values-Based Goals for Each Department**
6. Nakka encouraged departments to set goals that reflected not just performance but values. These goals became benchmarks of integrity, measures of success that honored their commitment to purpose.

Philosophical Reflection: Values as the Foundation of Resilience

In the quiet solitude of his office, Nakka reflected on the essence of values, on the nature of resilience. To him, values were more than ideals; they were the core, the heart of the organization. They were the foundation that anchored them, the strength that held them steady through change, through growth.

Resilience is not found in strength alone; it is found in purpose, he thought. *Values are the roots that ground us, the principles that allow us to endure.*

He believed that values were not meant to be convenient but challenging, commitments that tested them, that asked them to choose integrity over gain, purpose over expedience. In these choices, he saw their resilience, their ability to build something that would last.

The Impact of a Values-Driven Culture

Months passed, and Nakka saw the transformation. Employees acted with a new sense of purpose, a quiet confidence that came from knowing who they were, what they stood for. The values workshops, the recognition programs, the reflections—all had instilled a culture that was not only resilient but unified.

One day, he overheard a manager speaking to a new team member.

"Here, success is more than results. It's about integrity, about respecting our values. That's what makes us strong."

Nakka felt a deep satisfaction. His vision had taken root. The organization had become not just a workplace but a community, a place where values guided, where purpose strengthened. They were no longer driven by profit alone but by principles, by a commitment to a legacy that would endure.

Key Takeaways from Nakka's Approach to Building Resilience through Values

1. **Values as Action, Not Just Ideals**
2. Nakka's workshops and recognition programs turned values into actions, creating a culture where integrity, respect, and purpose were lived daily, not merely spoken.
3. **Reflection and Accountability as Anchors of Culture**
4. Through weekly reflections and decision-making frameworks, he reinforced accountability, reminding everyone that values were not optional but essential to their identity.
5. **Legacy of Integrity as the Measure of Success**
6. Nakka's conversations with leaders like Ramesh redefined success as a legacy, a foundation built on values that would endure, even as the organization grew.

7. **Shared Purpose as the Source of Resilience**
8. By aligning goals with values, Nakka created a culture where resilience came not from strength alone but from unity, from a shared commitment to integrity, to purpose.

Legacy of Nakka's Vision for a Values-Driven Culture

In the years that followed, the organization became known not just for its achievements but for its character. Employees felt a sense of belonging, a pride in their values, in the integrity that defined their work. The culture was resilient, a foundation that held firm even as they grew, as they faced new challenges.

Nakka's legacy was not merely a culture of values but a belief—that resilience was rooted in purpose, that integrity was the foundation of true success. He had shown them that values were not obstacles but strengths, that through commitment, they could build something that would endure.

Through his vision, Nakka had woven values into the heart of the organization, creating a legacy that was not only resilient but true, a testament to the power of purpose in building a culture that lasts.

Chapter 12

CRISIS MANAGEMENT – LEADERSHIP IN THE FACE OF UNCERTAINTY

Nakka's Belief: True Leadership Is Tested in the Fire of Crisis

The call came in the dead of night—a critical project had faltered, errors had compounded, and deadlines loomed with impossible urgency. The client was furious, contracts were on the line, and the organization's reputation hung by a thread. Nakka felt the weight of the moment, the responsibility that came with leadership in times of crisis.

To him, crisis was not merely a test of competence but of character. It was in these moments, he believed, that the essence of leadership was revealed. True leadership was not found in titles or authority but in the ability to stay anchored, to lead with calm, clarity, and resolve when everything around seemed uncertain.

In crisis, we reveal who we truly are, he thought. *It is a mirror that reflects our integrity, our resilience, our strength.*

A Conversation on Crisis with Senior Leaders

Nakka gathered his senior leaders to assess the situation. They spoke in tense tones, laying out facts, evaluating risks, discussing contingencies. Some voices rose, fraught with urgency, while others sank, weighed down by the magnitude of the challenge. He saw their anxiety, their fear of failure, but also their commitment, their determination to find a way through.

"What do you fear most in this crisis?" Nakka asked, his tone steady, his gaze intent.

One of the managers replied, "We fear losing the client's trust, damaging our reputation, maybe even facing legal consequences."

Nakka nodded, acknowledging the weight of their concerns. "Yes, these are real fears. But there is a deeper fear—the fear of losing ourselves, of compromising our values in pursuit of a solution. The true danger in crisis is not failure but the temptation to abandon integrity, to lose sight of who we are."

He paused, letting his words sink in. "We will solve this," he continued, his voice resolute. "But we will solve it without compromising our principles. Because if we lose our values, we lose everything."

Structured Response to Crisis: Actions and Protocols

Nakka understood that crisis management required both structure and adaptability. He knew that while each crisis was unique, a well-prepared organization could face uncertainty with confidence, turning fear into focused action.

Steps to Manage Crisis with Integrity and Clarity:

1. **Immediate Assessment and Root Cause Analysis**
2. Nakka prioritized an immediate assessment of the crisis. He assembled a team to analyze the root causes, to understand not just what had gone wrong but why. This approach allowed them to address the problem at its source, rather than merely treating symptoms.
3. **Crisis Communication Channels for Real-Time Updates**
4. He implemented dedicated communication channels, ensuring that every decision, every update reached the right people in real time. This clarity prevented miscommunication, aligning efforts and maintaining a unified response.
5. **Crisis Protocols Guided by Core Values**
6. Nakka established crisis protocols that were aligned with the organization's values. Each step, each decision was evaluated not only for its effectiveness but for its adherence to their principles, ensuring that their response was as ethical as it was efficient.

A Philosophical Exchange on Stability with Kavita, a Project Manager

During a moment of quiet in the midst of the crisis, Nakka spoke with Kavita, a project manager who had been visibly shaken by the events. She struggled with the fear that the situation was spiraling beyond control, that they were losing ground with each passing hour.

"Kavita," Nakka asked, his voice calm, "do you believe that stability is something we can control?"

She looked at him, her expression one of uncertainty. "I thought stability was... consistency, predictability. But right now, it feels like everything is out of control."

"Stability is not the absence of chaos," Nakka replied, his tone thoughtful. "It is the ability to stay anchored, to act with calm and purpose even when the world around us is in turmoil. Stability is not external—it is internal. It is the strength that comes from knowing who we are, from staying true to our values."

Kavita nodded, her perspective shifting. She saw now that stability was not in the situation but in their response, in their commitment to act with integrity, even in uncertainty.

Embedding Crisis Resilience Through Preparation and Reflection

Nakka knew that resilience in crisis was not built overnight. It required preparation, a readiness to face challenges without compromising principles. He implemented training sessions, simulations that allowed teams to practice crisis response, to build the confidence that would guide them when real challenges emerged.

Methods to Build Crisis Resilience:

1. **Crisis Simulations and Real-Time Drills**
2. Nakka introduced crisis simulations, realistic scenarios that challenged teams to respond with speed, clarity, and integrity. These drills became opportunities to test protocols, to reinforce the value of preparation.

3. **Post-Crisis Reflections for Continuous Improvement**
4. After each crisis, he held reflection sessions, where teams reviewed not only what they had done but how they had done it. These reflections became moments of learning, opportunities to improve both strategy and character.
5. **Values-Based Decision Training for Leaders**
6. He implemented training for leaders focused on values-based decision-making, preparing them to face crises with a commitment to integrity, ensuring that even in high-stakes situations, principles guided their actions.

Philosophical Reflection: Crisis as a Test of Integrity

In the silence of his office, Nakka reflected on the nature of crisis, on its role as both challenge and opportunity. To him, crisis was not merely an event but a crucible, a moment that tested not just their strength but their integrity. It was in these moments, he believed, that leadership was truly defined.

Integrity is not proven in ease but in adversity, he thought. *Crisis does not weaken us; it reveals our strength, our commitment to principles that do not waver.*

He knew that while crises would come and go, the integrity they upheld in each challenge would become part of the organization's identity, a legacy of resilience that would endure.

The Impact of Values-Driven Crisis Management

In the weeks following the crisis, Nakka saw the transformation in his team. They had faced the challenge with courage, with integrity. They had not only resolved the issue but had done so without compromising their principles. Clients recognized their commitment, their character, and the organization emerged from the crisis with a strengthened reputation.

One day, he overheard Kavita speaking to a new employee.

"In a crisis, we don't just focus on solutions. We focus on values, on staying true to who we are. That's what makes us strong."

Nakka felt a quiet pride. His vision had taken root. The organization was not only resilient but principled, prepared to face future crises with the same commitment to integrity, to purpose.

Key Takeaways from Nakka's Approach to Crisis Management

1. **Preparation as the Foundation of Crisis Resilience**
2. Through simulations and real-time drills, Nakka prepared his teams to face crises with confidence, building resilience that turned fear into focused action.
3. **Values as Anchors in Times of Uncertainty**
4. By aligning crisis protocols with core values, he ensured that integrity guided every decision, transforming crisis from a threat into an opportunity to demonstrate character.
5. **Reflection as a Tool for Growth and Learning**
6. Post-crisis reflections became moments of insight, reinforcing the organization's commitment to improvement, to growth, both in strategy and in spirit.
7. **Stability as Internal Strength, Not External Control**
8. Nakka's conversations with leaders like Kavita redefined stability as a state of mind, a strength that came from within, rooted in clarity and purpose.

Legacy of Nakka's Vision for Crisis Leadership

In the years that followed, the organization became known not only for its resilience but for its integrity in times of crisis. Employees felt a deep commitment to the organization's values, a trust in their leaders, a confidence that they would face any challenge with clarity and purpose.

Nakka's legacy was not merely a crisis protocol but a belief—that leadership was proven in adversity, that integrity was the foundation of true strength. He had shown them that crisis, far from being a threat, was an opportunity to uphold principles, to build a reputation rooted in character.

Through his vision, Nakka had woven resilience into the heart of the organization, creating a culture where crisis was not only managed but mastered, where values remained unshaken, a testament to the strength of leadership in the face of uncertainty.

Chapter 13

EMPLOYEE EMPOWERMENT – TRUSTING PEOPLE TO SUCCEED

Nakka's Philosophy: Empowerment Is the True Measure of Leadership

As Nakka observed his teams, he noticed a pattern—too often, decisions were held at the top, ideas were filtered, autonomy limited by layers of oversight. He saw the weight of bureaucracy pressing down on people, stifling their potential, curtailing their ability to act, to innovate. To him, this was not just a structural issue but a question of trust, a reluctance to believe in people's ability to rise to the occasion.

Nakka believed that empowerment was not a luxury but a necessity. A true leader, he thought, did not seek to control but to liberate. Real power was found not in authority but in trust, in the courage to let others take the lead, to make decisions, to learn, even to fail.

To lead is not to command but to trust, he thought. *Empowerment is not just permission; it is an invitation to succeed.*

A Dialogue on Trust with Shrey, a Mid-Level Manager

One afternoon, Nakka met with Shrey, a mid-level manager whose team had been struggling under the weight of his oversight. Shrey was diligent, committed, but Nakka sensed a hesitation in him, a reluctance to let go, to delegate.

"Shrey," Nakka began, his tone thoughtful, "do you trust your team?"

Shrey looked at him, slightly defensive. "Of course, I do. But… sometimes, they make mistakes, and I feel responsible for guiding them."

Nakka nodded, understanding. "Guidance is essential, yes. But do you believe that without room to decide, to learn, they can ever truly grow?"

Shrey hesitated, his defensiveness fading. "I suppose... I worry that if they fail, it reflects on me."

"But leadership is not about protecting yourself, Shrey," Nakka replied, his tone gentle but firm. "It is about empowering others, allowing them to discover their strengths, their abilities. Trust is not a shield; it is a bridge, an act of faith that brings out the best in people."

Shrey listened, a new understanding dawning in his eyes. He saw now that his fear of failure was not helping his team but hindering them, that true leadership required the courage to let others lead.

Empowering Through Autonomy: Steps and Structures

Determined to foster a culture of empowerment, Nakka implemented structures that promoted autonomy, that encouraged individuals to take ownership of their work, their decisions. He wanted empowerment not as an exception but as a standard, a culture where trust was the norm, not the reward.

Steps to Build an Empowering Culture:

1. **Delegation of Decision-Making Authority**
2. Nakka restructured roles to include decision-making authority, allowing employees to own their tasks fully. Each team member was given a sphere of influence, a space where their choices mattered, where their decisions drove progress.
3. **Empowerment Frameworks for Leaders**
4. He introduced frameworks for leaders, guidelines that encouraged them to delegate, to build trust. These frameworks weren't about relinquishing control but about creating opportunities for growth, moments where employees could act independently.
5. **Learning from Failure as a Tool for Growth**

6. Nakka created a culture that valued learning over perfection. Failure was not seen as a setback but as an experience, a lesson that strengthened resilience, that taught both leaders and employees to view mistakes as a natural part of growth.

A Philosophical Exchange on Responsibility with Naina, Head of Product Development

Nakka spoke with Naina, the head of Product Development, a leader known for her meticulous attention to detail. She struggled with delegation, often preferring to handle critical tasks herself, fearing that others might miss essential nuances.

"Naina," he asked, his voice soft but probing, "do you believe that perfection is necessary for success?"

She looked at him, thoughtful. "I suppose… I feel that each detail matters, that if something goes wrong, it reflects poorly on us all."

"But do you think that in holding onto every detail, you allow your team to grow, to succeed?"

Naina paused, understanding his point. "Perhaps I need to let go, to allow them the freedom to learn, even if it means mistakes."

"Yes," Nakka replied, his voice filled with conviction. "True empowerment is not about avoiding mistakes but about creating a culture where learning is valued, where growth is prioritized over perfection. We are not here to avoid failure, Naina. We are here to grow, to build resilience, to become stronger through trust."

She nodded, realizing that empowerment was an act of courage, a decision to believe in others, to trust them enough to allow their growth, their journey.

Building Empowerment into the Culture

Nakka took deliberate steps to embed empowerment into the organization's culture, creating practices that reinforced autonomy, that celebrated initiative. He wanted empowerment to be more than a concept; he wanted it to be a lived experience, a reality that strengthened the organization from within.

Methods to Foster a Culture of Empowerment:

1. **Regular Empowerment Check-Ins**
2. Nakka introduced regular empowerment check-ins, sessions where leaders and employees discussed autonomy, shared experiences, celebrated successes, and addressed challenges. These check-ins became spaces of trust, moments that reinforced the commitment to empowerment.
3. **Peer-Led Learning Sessions for Skill Sharing**
4. He established peer-led learning sessions, opportunities for employees to teach, to lead, to share their expertise with others. These sessions created a culture of shared growth, where empowerment was both given and received.
5. **Empowerment Awards to Celebrate Initiative**
6. Nakka introduced annual Empowerment Awards, recognizing employees who had demonstrated initiative, who had taken risks, who had grown through autonomy. These awards were a celebration of courage, of the freedom to act, to lead.

Philosophical Reflection: Empowerment as the Heart of Growth

In the quiet of his office, Nakka reflected on the nature of empowerment, on its role as both challenge and opportunity. To him, empowerment was more than autonomy; it was trust, a decision to believe in others, to see their potential, to invite them into their own success.

To empower is not to give away power but to give strength, he thought. *It is the courage to let go, to allow others to rise, to succeed on their terms.*

He believed that true empowerment was not found in commands but in encouragement, in the courage to see people as they could be, not as they were. In this belief, he found purpose—a purpose that guided his vision for the organization, a purpose that made empowerment a cornerstone of growth.

The Impact of a Culture of Empowerment

In the months that followed, Nakka saw the transformation within his teams. Employees acted with a newfound confidence, a sense of ownership that came from knowing they were trusted, valued. The regular check-ins, the learning sessions, the awards—all had fostered a culture where empowerment was not an exception but a standard.

One day, he overheard Shrey speaking to his team.

"Here, you're not just allowed to decide. You're encouraged to take the lead, to own your work. That's how we grow."

Nakka felt a deep satisfaction. His vision had taken root. The organization had become not just a place of work but a space of empowerment, a place where trust was given freely, where growth was encouraged, where each person was seen as capable, as worthy of autonomy.

Key Takeaways from Nakka's Approach to Employee Empowerment

1. **Trust as the Foundation of Autonomy**
2. Through delegation and frameworks, Nakka created a culture where trust was given, where autonomy was seen not as a reward but as a necessity for growth.
3. **Learning from Failure as a Path to Resilience**
4. By reframing failure as learning, he transformed mistakes into opportunities, building resilience and encouraging employees to see setbacks as steps toward strength.
5. **Celebration of Initiative as a Source of Motivation**
6. The Empowerment Awards and peer-led sessions fostered a sense of pride, creating a culture where initiative was celebrated, where empowerment was both given and received.
7. **Responsibility as a Shared Journey, Not a Burden**
8. Nakka's conversations with leaders like Naina redefined responsibility as shared, as a journey of growth rather than a burden of perfection.

Legacy of Nakka's Vision for Empowerment

In the years that followed, the organization became known not only for its achievements but for its trust in its people. Employees felt a deep connection, a sense of ownership, a pride in their autonomy. They were not just a workforce; they were empowered individuals, each a leader in their own right.

Nakka's legacy was not merely a culture of empowerment but a belief—that to lead was to trust, that true strength was found in the courage to let go. He had shown them that empowerment was not a gift but a foundation, a cornerstone of growth.

Through his vision, Nakka had woven empowerment into the heart of the organization, creating a culture where trust was the norm, where growth was encouraged, a testament to the power of believing in people, of inviting them to succeed.

Chapter 14

FEEDBACK – CONTINUOUS IMPROVEMENT

Nakka's Principle: Growth Is Rooted in the Courage to Receive and Give Truth

Nakka walked the halls of the organization, listening to the quiet hum of daily routines, the rhythm of tasks, the focus on productivity. But he sensed something else, something deeper—an unease, a reluctance among his team members to confront their own limitations, to seek growth in its truest form. He knew that the organization had grown skilled in routine, in achieving targets, but he wondered if they had grown skilled in the art of growth itself.

To Nakka, growth was not found in comfort, in praise alone, but in truth—truth shared honestly, with respect and purpose. Feedback, he believed, was not a correction but an invitation to improve, a dialogue that allowed each person to become more than they were.

Growth demands courage, he thought. *The courage to see ourselves clearly, to accept both praise and correction with an open heart.*

A Conversation on Feedback with Leela, a Rising Team Leader

One afternoon, Nakka met with Leela, a promising team leader who had begun to excel in her role. She was diligent, talented, but Nakka sensed a quiet reluctance within her—a fear of criticism, a tendency to seek only affirmation.

"Leela," he asked gently, "what does feedback mean to you?"

She hesitated, her expression guarded. "I suppose… it's a way to improve. But sometimes, it feels like criticism, like it's pointing out my flaws."

Nakka nodded, understanding her perspective. "Feedback can feel that way, yes. But have you ever considered that feedback is a mirror, a reflection that shows both our strengths and our areas for growth?"

Leela looked at him thoughtfully. "I hadn't thought of it that way."

"Growth requires that we see ourselves honestly," Nakka continued, his tone steady. "Feedback is not judgment; it is a gift, an opportunity to become better. But it requires courage—the courage to accept what is hard to hear, to use it as fuel for improvement."

Leela listened, a shift in her expression. She realized that feedback was not a measure of failure but a path to becoming more capable, more resilient, more herself.

Establishing Feedback as a Culture of Growth

Determined to foster a culture where feedback was seen as a tool for improvement rather than a critique, Nakka introduced systems and practices that encouraged open dialogue, mutual respect, and a commitment to continuous growth.

Steps to Embed Feedback as a Core Value:

1. **Introduction of Continuous Feedback Loops**
2. Nakka implemented a continuous feedback system that allowed feedback to be given regularly, rather than reserved for annual reviews. This system created a rhythm of growth, an ongoing conversation that emphasized improvement as a constant journey.
3. **360-Degree Feedback to Foster Holistic Insights**
4. He introduced 360-degree feedback, allowing team members to receive insights not only from managers but also from peers, subordinates, and cross-functional teams. This holistic approach helped individuals see a fuller picture, creating a culture where feedback was shared openly, respectfully.

5. **Feedback Training to Encourage Honest, Constructive Dialogue**
6. Nakka organized training sessions on how to give and receive feedback constructively. He wanted feedback to be delivered with respect, received with openness, fostering a culture where both the giver and receiver saw feedback as a partnership in growth.

A Philosophical Exchange on Truth with Arun, Head of Sales

Nakka sought out Arun, the head of Sales, a man known for his results-driven approach but sometimes resistant to feedback that challenged his methods. Nakka wanted him to see feedback not as criticism but as an ally, a friend that revealed truth.

"Arun," he asked, his tone contemplative, "do you think truth is something we should only seek when it is comfortable?"

Arun's gaze was cautious. "I suppose… no. But truth can be hard. It can… hurt."

"Yes, it can," Nakka replied, his voice steady. "But would you rather live comfortably in a half-truth or grow through the discomfort of seeing clearly?"

Arun paused, considering this. "I suppose… growth requires that we face reality, even when it is difficult."

"Exactly," Nakka nodded. "Feedback is truth. It is not meant to hurt but to help, to guide us toward our potential. We must not fear it but welcome it, knowing that through it, we become stronger, more capable, more ourselves."

Arun listened, realizing now that feedback was not an intrusion but an invitation to see beyond his comfort, to grow into his potential.

Creating a Feedback-Driven Culture

Nakka took steps to weave feedback into the fabric of the organization, not as a duty but as a gift, a shared commitment to excellence. He wanted feedback to become a part of the organization's language, a culture where improvement was a constant, valued pursuit.

Methods to Normalize Feedback as a Daily Practice:

1. **Weekly Reflection Sessions for Team-Based Feedback**
2. Nakka introduced weekly reflection sessions where teams discussed both successes and areas for growth. These sessions were spaces for open dialogue, where feedback was seen as collaboration, not correction.
3. **Mentorship Programs to Encourage Feedback in Development**
4. He established mentorship programs that included feedback as a core component. Mentors guided mentees not only in tasks but in growth, sharing insights that helped them navigate challenges, realize potential.
5. **Celebration of Growth as a Result of Feedback**
6. Nakka introduced a "Growth Award" that celebrated individuals who had demonstrated exceptional improvement through feedback. This award honored not just performance but the courage to embrace feedback, to grow through truth.

Philosophical Reflection: Feedback as a Journey of Becoming

In the solitude of his office, Nakka reflected on the nature of feedback, on its role as both teacher and guide. To him, feedback was not just a tool but a journey, a path that invited each person to become more than they were, to see themselves clearly and courageously.

Feedback is not about what we are but what we can become, he thought. *It is a mirror that reveals our potential, a bridge between comfort and growth.*

He believed that feedback was not meant to judge but to elevate, that it required both humility and strength. In this belief, he found clarity—a clarity that allowed him to guide the organization toward a culture where growth was a shared journey, a commitment to continuous improvement.

The Impact of a Feedback-Driven Culture

In the months that followed, Nakka saw the transformation within his teams. Employees engaged in feedback conversations openly, their responses marked by curiosity, by the courage to improve. The reflection sessions, the mentorships, the growth awards—all had nurtured a culture where feedback was not a burden but a privilege.

One day, he overheard Leela speaking to a colleague.

"Feedback here isn't just criticism. It's guidance. It's the way we become better, stronger."

Nakka felt a quiet pride. His vision had taken root. The organization had become a place where feedback was not feared but welcomed, a space where truth was valued, where each person's growth was a journey shared, celebrated.

Key Takeaways from Nakka's Approach to Feedback and Continuous Improvement

1. **Feedback as an Invitation to Growth**
2. Through continuous feedback loops and 360-degree insights, Nakka established a culture where feedback was a tool for improvement, an invitation to grow, to see clearly.
3. **Truth as a Path to Excellence**
4. Nakka's conversations with leaders like Arun redefined feedback as truth, as a bridge to potential, creating a culture where feedback was valued, not resisted.
5. **Courage and Humility as Pillars of Growth**
6. Through training and mentorship, he instilled the value of courage in receiving feedback, of humility in giving it, fostering a culture where both roles were honored.
7. **Celebration of Growth as a Source of Motivation**
8. The Growth Award celebrated the courage to improve, to grow through feedback, creating a culture where growth was not only valued but celebrated.

Legacy of Nakka's Vision for Feedback-Driven Growth

In the years that followed, the organization became known not only for its achievements but for its commitment to growth. Employees felt a deep connection to their development, a pride in their journey, a belief in their potential. They were not just team members; they were individuals on a path of continuous improvement, each becoming more than they were.

Nakka's legacy was not merely a culture of feedback but a belief—that growth was rooted in truth, that feedback was a gift that required both courage and humility. He had shown them that feedback was not a burden but a path, a journey toward excellence.

Through his vision, Nakka had woven feedback into the heart of the organization, creating a culture where growth was celebrated, where truth was honored, a testament to the power of continuous improvement, to the courage to become.

Chapter 15

SUSTAINABILITY AND CORPORATE SOCIAL RESPONSIBILITY – BEYOND PROFIT

Nakka's Vision: Success Must Serve a Purpose Greater Than Profit

Nakka stood in the quiet of his office, reflecting on the company's recent financial gains, the growth that had marked their journey. Yet, as he looked out at the city beyond, he felt a nagging unease, a sense that something was missing. Growth, profit—these were important, but were they enough? He believed that a business should be more than a machine for profit, more than an engine for its own gain.

To Nakka, true success was measured not in revenue alone but in the impact they left on the world, the legacy they built for those who would come after. He believed that a company, like an individual, had a responsibility—not only to itself but to the society it served, the environment it affected.

Success is not defined by what we take from the world but by what we give back, he thought. *True leadership considers both profit and purpose, growth and responsibility.*

A Conversation on Purpose with Tanvi, Head of Corporate Strategy

Nakka called a meeting with Tanvi, the head of Corporate Strategy, a sharp, ambitious leader who had driven much of the organization's growth. She was focused, committed, but he sensed a disconnect—a focus on short-term gains, on metrics alone.

"Tanvi," he began, his voice calm, "do you believe that profit is the only measure of our success?"

She looked at him, momentarily taken aback. "Well… profit is essential. Without it, we can't grow, can't sustain ourselves."

Nakka nodded. "Yes, profit is essential. But does it fulfill our purpose? Does it leave the world better than we found it?"

Tanvi considered this, realizing the depth of his question. "I suppose… I've focused so much on results that I haven't thought about our impact beyond the bottom line."

"We have a duty, Tanvi," he continued, his tone resolute. "A duty to consider the world we affect—the communities we touch, the environment we use. Success should not come at the expense of the world. It should elevate, improve, create. That is our true legacy."

Tanvi listened, understanding now that profit was a part of their purpose but not its entirety. She saw that true success was broader, deeper, encompassing not only their gains but their impact.

Integrating Purpose into Profit: Actions and Initiatives

Determined to root corporate responsibility and sustainability within the organization, Nakka launched initiatives that prioritized impact, that aligned their growth with ethical, sustainable practices. He wanted the organization to become a force for good, a company that achieved not just for itself but for the world.

Steps to Align Success with Sustainability:

1. **Creation of a Sustainability and CSR Committee**
2. Nakka established a dedicated committee focused on sustainability and corporate social responsibility. This team became the organization's conscience, ensuring that every decision, every project considered environmental and social impact.
3. **Environmental Initiatives Focused on Minimizing Impact**
4. He introduced programs aimed at reducing waste, conserving resources, and offsetting carbon emissions. From eco-friendly materials to renewable energy sources, every choice reflected a commitment to sustainability, to a legacy that respected the environment.

5. **Community Engagement Programs to Give Back**
6. Nakka launched initiatives that encouraged employees to engage with local communities, to volunteer, to contribute their skills and time. These programs became more than service; they became connections, relationships that bridged the gap between the company and the world around it.

A Philosophical Dialogue on Legacy with Veer, CFO

Nakka sat down with Veer, the Chief Financial Officer, a man deeply invested in metrics, in growth forecasts. Veer was dedicated to the company's financial health, but Nakka wanted him to see beyond numbers, to consider the ethical impact of every financial decision.

"Veer," he asked, his tone thoughtful, "do you think our legacy is found in the numbers we leave behind?"

Veer looked at him, slightly puzzled. "Isn't financial success… what defines a company's legacy?"

"Financial success is part of it, yes," Nakka replied. "But if we succeed financially yet fail ethically, if we grow in revenue but diminish in responsibility—what kind of legacy is that?"

Veer paused, realizing the weight of Nakka's words. "I suppose… a legacy that is only profitable is incomplete. It doesn't… give back."

"Exactly," Nakka said, his gaze intent. "Our legacy is measured not only by profit but by purpose. We must build something that serves the world, that leaves it better. Success is incomplete if it serves only ourselves."

Veer nodded, understanding now that his role was not only to manage finances but to ensure that every decision reflected the organization's ethical commitment, its responsibility to society, to the future.

Building Responsibility into the Organization's DNA

Nakka took steps to embed corporate responsibility into the culture, creating practices that aligned growth with impact, profit with purpose. He wanted sustainability not as an initiative but as a core value, a shared belief that guided every choice, every action.

Methods to Foster Corporate Responsibility:

1. **Annual Impact Reports to Measure and Reflect**
2. Nakka introduced annual impact reports, transparent assessments of the organization's environmental and social contributions. These reports became moments of reflection, accountability, reminders that their impact was measured not only in profits but in purpose.
3. **Sustainability Goals Aligned with Business Objectives**
4. He set sustainability goals that were as prioritized as revenue targets. These goals became benchmarks of ethical growth, indicators of success that honored both profit and responsibility.
5. **Employee-Led Social Responsibility Programs**
6. Nakka encouraged employees to lead social responsibility initiatives, fostering a sense of ownership, of pride. These programs created a culture where giving back was not a duty but a privilege, a reflection of shared values.

Philosophical Reflection: Sustainability as the Heart of Legacy

In the stillness of his office, Nakka reflected on the nature of legacy, on the essence of responsibility. To him, sustainability was not merely environmental; it was existential, a question of purpose. He believed that a company, like a person, must consider its impact, must measure success not only in gain but in goodness.

Legacy is not built in wealth alone; it is built in worth, he thought. *Our true success is found not in what we take but in what we give, in the world we leave behind.*

He believed that sustainability was not a strategy but a commitment, a way of living that honored both present and future. In this belief, he found resolve—a resolve that guided his vision for the organization, a purpose that transcended profit.

The Impact of a Responsibility-Driven Culture

In the months that followed, Nakka saw the transformation within his teams. Employees acted with a new sense of purpose, a commitment to making choices that honored both profit and the planet. The CSR committee, the impact reports, the community engagement—all had nurtured a culture where responsibility was not an add-on but a foundation.

One day, he overheard Tanvi speaking to her team.

"Here, success isn't just about profit. It's about purpose. We don't just grow for ourselves; we grow for the world."

Nakka felt a quiet pride. His vision had taken root. The organization had become a place where success was measured in impact, where responsibility was honored, where each person saw their role as a contributor to a greater good.

Key Takeaways from Nakka's Approach to Corporate Responsibility

1. **Purpose Beyond Profit as the Measure of Success**
2. Through the CSR committee and environmental initiatives, Nakka created a culture where success was measured in both growth and impact, where purpose defined their legacy.
3. **Transparency and Accountability as Pillars of Responsibility**
4. The annual impact reports and sustainability goals held the organization accountable, ensuring that every achievement honored both profit and planet.
5. **Community Engagement as a Bridge to the World**
6. The community programs fostered a connection between the organization and society, building a legacy that was not just profitable but purposeful.
7. **Employee Ownership of Responsibility as a Source of Pride**
8. By empowering employees to lead social initiatives, Nakka created a culture where responsibility was shared, where giving back was a source of pride, of purpose.

Legacy of Nakka's Vision for Sustainability and Responsibility

In the years that followed, the organization became known not only for its success but for its purpose, its commitment to a legacy that honored both profit and planet. Employees felt a deep connection to their work, a pride in their impact, a belief in their role as contributors to a better world. They were not just part of a company; they were part of a movement for good.

Nakka's legacy was not merely a culture of responsibility but a belief—that true success was found in impact, that legacy was measured in purpose. He had shown them that sustainability was not a sacrifice but a strength, a path to a legacy that would endure.

Through his vision, Nakka had woven responsibility into the heart of the organization, creating a culture where growth served not only themselves but the world, a testament to the power of purpose in building a legacy that lasts.

Chapter 16

SUCCESSION PLANNING – PREPARING THE NEXT GENERATION

Nakka's Legacy: True Leadership Prepares Others to Carry the Torch Forward

As Nakka walked the familiar corridors of the company he had helped shape, he felt both pride and a quiet unease. He knew his time here was finite, that every leader must eventually step aside, making room for new voices, new perspectives. But he also believed that leadership was not a solitary journey. True leadership, he thought, was measured not in accomplishments but in the ability to prepare others, to cultivate a generation that could carry the vision forward with strength, integrity, and innovation.

To Nakka, succession planning was more than a strategic necessity; it was a philosophical duty. A legacy was not a moment frozen in time; it was a bridge to the future, a foundation that evolved, that was strengthened by the people who inherited it. He believed that in preparing future leaders, he was not just preserving the organization's future but empowering it to grow, to become more than he had imagined.

The measure of a leader is not in the power they wield but in the strength they leave behind, he thought. *True leadership is about continuity, about building a legacy that endures beyond oneself.*

A Discussion on Legacy with Mira, an Emerging Leader

One afternoon, Nakka sat with Mira, a young and ambitious manager who had shown great promise. She was eager, committed, yet he sensed an uncertainty in her—a fear that she might not be ready to lead, to step into his shoes.

"Mira," he began gently, "what does legacy mean to you?"

She hesitated, then spoke thoughtfully. "I suppose… legacy is what we leave behind. It's the mark we make."

Nakka nodded, a faint smile on his lips. "Yes, legacy is what we leave. But more than that, it is what we give. Legacy is not just a mark; it is a foundation, a strength that others build upon. It is a gift that must be nurtured, protected, and, most importantly, passed on."

Mira listened, understanding now that her role was not only to succeed but to prepare others, to become a link in the chain of continuity.

"Leadership is not about holding on to power," he continued, his voice steady. "It is about creating new leaders, people who will one day take our place, who will carry our values forward, even beyond our time here."

Structuring Succession as a Culture of Continuity

Determined to create a structured approach to succession, Nakka implemented practices that identified, developed, and mentored emerging leaders within the organization. He wanted succession to be more than a plan—it was to become a culture, a commitment to continuity that every leader upheld.

Steps to Build a Sustainable Succession Framework:

1. **Early Identification of Potential Leaders**
2. Nakka introduced a system to identify high-potential employees early in their careers. Through careful observation and mentorship, he sought to recognize those who showed not only skill but character, a commitment to values and to growth.
3. **Structured Mentorship Programs to Guide Development**

4. He established formal mentorship programs, pairing experienced leaders with emerging talents. This mentorship was more than guidance; it was a relationship, a partnership in growth that prepared mentees not only for tasks but for the challenges of leadership.

5. **Challenging Assignments to Foster Growth**

6. Nakka encouraged managers to give promising employees challenging assignments, "stretch" roles that would push them beyond their comfort zones. These assignments were tests, experiences that taught resilience, that built confidence and skill.

A Philosophical Exchange on Responsibility with Akash, Director of Operations

Nakka met with Akash, the Director of Operations, a seasoned leader who had grown comfortable in his role, who had begun to resist change. Nakka wanted him to see that leadership was not about preservation but evolution, about passing the torch, preparing others to step forward.

"Akash," he asked, his tone steady, "do you believe that leadership is something we can hold on to forever?"

Akash looked at him, thoughtful. "I suppose... I thought leadership was about consistency, about ensuring that our systems stay strong."

"Yes, consistency is vital," Nakka replied, his voice reflective. "But if we hold on too tightly, if we do not prepare others, we become the barrier to progress, to growth. Leadership is not an ownership; it is a responsibility. Our duty is not to stay but to prepare, to build a legacy that others can carry forward."

Akash listened, realizing now that his role was not only to maintain but to mentor, to become part of a continuum that empowered new leaders, that ensured the organization would thrive beyond his tenure.

Embedding Succession into the Organization's DNA

Nakka took steps to make succession planning an integral part of the organization's culture, a shared responsibility that each leader carried. He wanted succession to be seen not as a departure but as a foundation, a structure that supported the growth and resilience of the organization.

Methods to Foster a Culture of Succession:

1. **Annual Leadership Development Summits**
2. Nakka introduced annual summits where leaders discussed succession strategies, shared insights on mentoring, on identifying potential. These summits became spaces of learning, moments where leaders committed to building a legacy through others.
3. **Succession Metrics and Goals for Each Department**
4. He implemented succession metrics, setting goals for each department to develop future leaders, to ensure that every role, every skill, was prepared to be passed on. These metrics became benchmarks of continuity, of a culture that valued legacy.
5. **Celebrating Leadership Transitions as Milestones**
6. Nakka introduced the concept of celebrating transitions, treating each leadership handover as a milestone, a moment of continuity that was honored, respected. These celebrations became reminders that leadership was not lost but shared, that each transition strengthened the organization.

Philosophical Reflection: Succession as a Gift of Continuity

In the quiet moments of reflection, Nakka considered the nature of succession, of legacy. To him, succession was not an end but a beginning, a new chapter written by the hands of those who had been prepared, mentored, empowered to lead.

Legacy is not built in what we achieve alone but in what we give, he thought. *True leadership is not an ownership but a gift, a strength that is passed forward.*

He believed that succession was an act of generosity, of faith in the future, a testament to the belief that the organization's vision was greater than any one individual. In this belief, he found purpose—a purpose that guided his commitment to build leaders, to create a legacy that would endure.

The Impact of a Succession-Driven Culture

In the months that followed, Nakka saw the transformation within his teams. Emerging leaders stepped into new roles with confidence, guided by mentors who had become their allies, their advocates. The leadership summits, the metrics, the celebrations—all had nurtured a culture where succession was not a departure but a continuity, a strength passed from one generation to the next.

One day, he overheard Mira speaking to a colleague.

"Here, leadership isn't just about our role; it's about preparing others. We don't just lead; we create leaders."

Nakka felt a quiet pride. His vision had taken root. The organization had become a place where leadership was not held tightly but shared, a place where each leader became a part of a legacy, a commitment to continuity.

Key Takeaways from Nakka's Approach to Succession Planning

1. **Leadership as a Responsibility to Build Others**
2. Through mentorship and challenging assignments, Nakka created a culture where leadership was not about power but about preparing others, creating a legacy of strength.
3. **Continuity as a Core Value, Not an Afterthought**
4. Nakka's summits and metrics embedded succession into the organization's DNA, making continuity a shared responsibility, a commitment that every leader honored.
5. **Celebration of Transitions as Affirmations of Growth**
6. The leadership transitions became celebrations, reminders that succession was not an ending but a beginning, a strengthening of the organization's foundation.

7. **Generosity and Faith as Pillars of True Leadership**
8. Nakka's conversations with leaders like Akash redefined leadership as an act of generosity, a trust in the future that valued continuity over permanence.

Legacy of Nakka's Vision for Succession and Continuity

In the years that followed, the organization became known not only for its achievements but for its commitment to continuity, to the leaders it built, to the legacy it nurtured. Employees felt a deep connection to the organization's vision, a pride in their role as part of a legacy that would outlast them. They were not just leaders; they were builders of the future.

Nakka's legacy was not merely a culture of succession but a belief—that leadership was a gift, that continuity was a strength. He had shown them that succession was not a loss but a gain, a path to resilience, to an organization that would endure.

Through his vision, Nakka had woven succession into the heart of the organization, creating a culture where leadership was shared, where legacy was honored, a testament to the power of preparing the next generation, of building a future that would thrive.

Chapter 17

ADAPTABILITY – EMBRACING CHANGE AS A STRENGTH

Nakka's Belief: Adaptability Is the Core of Resilience

Nakka knew that in the world of business, change was inevitable—markets shifted, technologies evolved, and customer needs grew complex. He had watched countless organizations struggle against change, clinging to familiar ways even as the world transformed around them. But to him, resistance to change was a weakness, a refusal to grow. He believed that adaptability was more than flexibility; it was a strength, a mindset that turned uncertainty into opportunity.

Change is not a disruption, he thought. *It is an invitation to adapt, to innovate, to become.*

For Nakka, adaptability was not merely a response to external pressures; it was a core value, a way of embracing the unknown with curiosity and courage. He believed that by fostering adaptability, the organization could not only survive but thrive, becoming stronger with each change, more resilient with every challenge.

A Conversation on Change with Anil, a Veteran Manager

One day, Nakka met with Anil, a senior manager who had been with the organization since its early days. Anil was loyal, experienced, but Nakka sensed a reluctance in him, a fear of the new technologies and strategies that were reshaping their industry.

"Anil," Nakka asked gently, "what does change mean to you?"

Anil hesitated, his gaze thoughtful. "I suppose... it feels like losing what we've built. Like we're letting go of our history, our foundation."

Nakka nodded, understanding his perspective. "But is change truly a loss, or could it be an evolution?"

Anil looked at him, uncertain. "I hadn't thought of it that way. But if we change too much… do we lose who we are?"

"We don't lose ourselves by changing," Nakka replied, his tone calm but firm. "We become more ourselves. Adaptability is not about abandoning the past but about carrying our values forward, growing stronger with each transformation."

Anil listened, realizing that adaptability was not a threat but an ally, a way to honor their legacy by building on it, by moving forward with strength and purpose.

Building Adaptability into the Culture

Determined to make adaptability a core organizational strength, Nakka introduced practices that encouraged open-mindedness, resilience, and a willingness to embrace change as an opportunity for growth. He wanted adaptability to become more than a reaction; he wanted it to be a proactive mindset, a readiness to evolve.

Steps to Foster a Culture of Adaptability:

1. **Change-Readiness Workshops and Training**
2. Nakka implemented workshops focused on adaptability, training employees to see change as a positive force. These sessions taught resilience, flexibility, and the skills needed to pivot, to innovate when faced with new challenges.
3. **Open Dialogue on Change and Innovation**
4. He created spaces where employees could openly discuss changes, ask questions, express concerns. These dialogues became opportunities to share ideas, to build a collective understanding that change was a shared journey, not an imposed directive.
5. **Pilot Programs for Testing New Ideas**
6. Nakka encouraged teams to launch pilot programs, to experiment with new processes, technologies, and strategies on a smaller scale before full implementation. These pilots became incubators of innovation, places where adaptability was practiced, refined, strengthened.

A Philosophical Dialogue on Resilience with Saira, Head of Technology

Nakka spoke with Saira, the Head of Technology, a visionary who had led many of the organization's recent innovations but often struggled to bring her team along with her. She was passionate but sometimes frustrated by the resistance she encountered.

"Saira," he asked, his voice thoughtful, "do you think resilience is about standing firm, or is it about the ability to bend without breaking?"

She looked at him, considering his question. "I always thought resilience was... strength, holding on, staying strong."

"Strength is part of it," Nakka replied, his gaze intent. "But true resilience is flexibility, the courage to adapt, to change shape without losing essence. Resilience is not a wall; it's a river that flows, finds new paths, always moving forward."

Saira listened, understanding now that resilience was not about resistance but adaptability, that her role was not to push against reluctance but to guide, to encourage flexibility, to lead by example.

Embedding Adaptability into the Organization's DNA

Nakka took steps to weave adaptability into the fabric of the organization, creating practices and structures that made change not only manageable but inspiring. He wanted adaptability to become a shared strength, a value that empowered everyone to see change as an opportunity.

Methods to Normalize Adaptability:

1. **Annual Innovation Days to Explore New Ideas**
2. Nakka introduced Innovation Days, annual events where teams came together to explore new technologies, brainstorm strategies, and test fresh ideas. These days became celebrations of change, reminders that adaptability was a source of creativity and growth.
3. **Cross-Functional Teams for Collaborative Problem Solving**
4. He established cross-functional teams to address challenges, bringing together diverse perspectives to create adaptive solutions. These teams encouraged collaboration, turning adaptability into a collective effort.

5. **Celebrating Successful Adaptations as Milestones**

6. Nakka introduced the concept of celebrating successful adaptations, honoring teams that had navigated change with resilience, that had embraced new methods with open minds. These celebrations became affirmations that change was not only possible but positive.

Philosophical Reflection: Adaptability as the Heart of Growth

In the quiet moments of reflection, Nakka considered the nature of adaptability, of change. To him, adaptability was more than flexibility; it was a belief, a faith in the organization's ability to evolve, to grow stronger with each new challenge.

Adaptability is not a compromise but a strength, he thought. *It is the courage to face the unknown, to transform without losing essence.*

He believed that adaptability was not about abandoning stability but about finding strength within change, about becoming resilient in the face of uncertainty. In this belief, he found purpose—a purpose that guided his vision for a future where change was not feared but embraced.

The Impact of an Adaptable Culture

In the months that followed, Nakka saw the transformation within his teams. Employees approached change with curiosity, with a willingness to explore new paths. The Innovation Days, the pilot programs, the cross-functional teams—all had nurtured a culture where adaptability was not only accepted but celebrated.

One day, he overheard Anil speaking to a new hire.

"Here, we don't resist change. We embrace it, because every change is a chance to grow."

Nakka felt a quiet pride. His vision had taken root. The organization had become a place where adaptability was a shared strength, where resilience was found not in resistance but in openness, in a collective commitment to growth.

Key Takeaways from Nakka's Approach to Adaptability

1. **Adaptability as a Core Value, Not a Reaction**
2. Through change-readiness training and Innovation Days, Nakka created a culture where adaptability was proactive, a mindset that embraced change as a strength.
3. **Resilience Through Flexibility, Not Resistance**
4. Nakka's conversations with leaders like Saira redefined resilience as the ability to adapt, to evolve without losing essence, creating a culture where flexibility was celebrated.
5. **Collective Adaptation Through Collaboration**
6. The cross-functional teams fostered a collective approach to change, making adaptability a shared journey, a strength built through collaboration.
7. **Celebration of Change as a Source of Growth**
8. By honoring successful adaptations, Nakka reinforced the idea that change was not an obstacle but an opportunity, a path to becoming stronger, more innovative.

Legacy of Nakka's Vision for Adaptability

In the years that followed, the organization became known not only for its stability but for its adaptability, its strength in the face of change. Employees felt a deep connection to the organization's journey, a pride in their role as agents of growth, a belief in their ability to evolve. They were not just part of a team; they were pioneers of a future built on resilience.

Nakka's legacy was not merely a culture of adaptability but a belief—that change was a gift, that resilience was found in flexibility. He had shown them that adaptability was not a compromise but a strength, a path to a future that thrived.

Through his vision, Nakka had woven adaptability into the heart of the organization, creating a culture where change was welcomed, where growth was embraced, a testament to the power of resilience, to the courage to adapt.

Chapter 18

TRANSPARENCY – BUILDING TRUST THROUGH OPENNESS

Nakka's Conviction: Trust Is Built on a Foundation of Truth

Nakka had always believed that honesty was not simply a virtue—it was a necessity, a cornerstone upon which all relationships, all progress, were built. In his mind, transparency was more than a policy; it was a commitment, a principle that held the organization together, that gave each person a sense of place, of purpose. He understood that without transparency, there could be no trust, and without trust, an organization was little more than a hollow structure.

Transparency is not about sharing every detail; it is about building trust, he thought. *It is the courage to be seen, to be understood, to be accountable.*

For Nakka, transparency was the highest form of respect, a way of honoring people by sharing truth, by inviting them into the story of the organization. He believed that when people were given truth, they responded with commitment, with loyalty, with a sense of shared ownership.

A Conversation on Trust with Ravi, the Communications Director

One afternoon, Nakka met with Ravi, the organization's Communications Director, a man skilled in crafting messages but often hesitant to reveal too much, fearing that transparency might lead to misunderstanding or even vulnerability.

"Ravi," Nakka began, his tone calm, "what does transparency mean to you?"

Ravi looked thoughtful. "I suppose… it's about being honest, but also careful. Sometimes, too much openness can lead to confusion, even misinterpretation."

Nakka nodded, understanding the delicate balance. "Yes, openness requires thought. But is trust possible if we hold back, if we decide that others cannot handle the truth?"

Ravi hesitated, considering this. "Perhaps… I worry that transparency might be risky, that it could create issues rather than solve them."

"Transparency is a risk, yes," Nakka agreed, his voice resolute. "But it is a necessary one. Trust cannot thrive on secrecy. To build trust, we must give truth, even when it is difficult. Transparency is not a weakness; it is a strength, a choice to trust others with what matters."

Ravi listened, understanding now that transparency was not about revealing everything but about sharing what was meaningful, about building trust through honesty.

Embedding Transparency as a Cultural Standard

Determined to root transparency within the organization, Nakka introduced practices that fostered open communication, accountability, and a shared sense of trust. He wanted transparency to become more than a policy; he wanted it to be a promise, a culture of openness that everyone respected.

Steps to Create a Culture of Transparency:

1. **Regular Town Halls and Open Forums**
2. Nakka introduced regular town halls where leadership openly discussed the organization's goals, challenges, and progress. These sessions allowed employees to ask questions, to engage with leadership, creating a direct line of communication that reinforced trust.

3. **Transparent Metrics and Performance Reports**
4. He implemented open access to key metrics, allowing employees to see the organization's progress, its setbacks, its growth. This transparency fostered accountability, ensuring that everyone was aligned, that everyone felt included in the journey.
5. **Feedback Channels for Open Communication**
6. Nakka established feedback channels where employees could share concerns, suggestions, and questions anonymously if needed. These channels became spaces of trust, allowing voices to be heard without fear, creating a culture where transparency was both given and received.

A Philosophical Exchange on Honesty with Priya, Head of Human Resources

Nakka met with Priya, the head of HR, a leader committed to fairness but often cautious about revealing too much, especially regarding sensitive issues. Nakka wanted her to see transparency not as a liability but as a way to build connection, to strengthen trust.

"Priya," he asked, his tone thoughtful, "do you think honesty is a burden, or could it be a bond?"

Priya looked at him, a faint smile on her lips. "I suppose… I've always thought honesty was a risk, that it needed to be managed carefully."

"Honesty does carry risk," Nakka replied, his gaze intent. "But without it, we create distance. Trust requires honesty, even when it is uncomfortable. Transparency is not about revealing everything; it is about sharing enough to build connection, to create a bond that cannot be broken by doubt."

Priya listened, realizing now that honesty was not a threat but a bridge, that transparency was not a liability but a foundation of trust.

Making Transparency a Foundation of the Organization

Nakka took steps to make transparency an integral part of the organization's culture, creating practices that built trust through openness, accountability, and mutual respect. He wanted transparency to be a shared value, a commitment that everyone honored.

Methods to Foster a Culture of Transparency:

1. **Monthly Leadership Q&A Sessions for Direct Dialogue**
2. Nakka introduced monthly Q&A sessions where employees could speak directly with leadership, ask questions, share concerns. These sessions created a culture of accessibility, a reminder that transparency was about dialogue, about listening.
3. **Transparent Decision-Making Processes**
4. He established clear decision-making processes that were visible to all. Employees understood how and why decisions were made, creating a sense of inclusion, of trust in the organization's direction.
5. **Celebrating Openness as a Value**
6. Nakka introduced annual recognition for employees who exemplified openness, who encouraged transparent practices. This recognition celebrated transparency as a strength, a shared commitment to truth.

Philosophical Reflection: Transparency as the Heart of Trust

In the solitude of his office, Nakka reflected on the nature of transparency, on its role in building connection. To him, transparency was not about disclosure but about building trust, about creating relationships rooted in truth, in respect.

Transparency is not a risk but a strength, he thought. *It is the courage to trust others with truth, to build a foundation that no doubt can shake.*

He believed that transparency was not about what was revealed but about what was shared, that it was a bridge between individuals, a commitment to connection. In this belief, he found purpose—a purpose that guided his vision for an organization where trust was built on openness.

The Impact of a Transparent Culture

In the months that followed, Nakka saw the transformation within his teams. Employees engaged openly, trusted leadership, felt a connection to the organization's vision. The town halls, the open metrics, the feedback channels—all had nurtured a culture where transparency was not only respected but valued.

One day, he overheard Ravi speaking to his team.

"Here, we don't just communicate. We share. We believe that openness builds trust."

Nakka felt a quiet pride. His vision had taken root. The organization had become a place where transparency was the foundation of every relationship, where trust was not demanded but earned, where each person felt valued, seen, respected.

Key Takeaways from Nakka's Approach to Transparency

1. **Transparency as the Foundation of Trust**
2. Through town halls and accessible metrics, Nakka created a culture where transparency was a shared commitment, where trust was built on openness.
3. **Honesty as a Bridge, Not a Burden**
4. Nakka's conversations with leaders like Priya redefined transparency as a bond, a bridge that strengthened trust, creating a culture where truth was respected.
5. **Accountability Through Openness**
6. The open decision-making processes fostered accountability, making transparency a foundation of shared responsibility, a commitment to truth.
7. **Celebration of Openness as a Shared Value**
8. By honoring transparency, Nakka reinforced the idea that openness was not a risk but a strength, a foundation of trust, a culture of mutual respect.

Legacy of Nakka's Vision for Transparency

In the years that followed, the organization became known not only for its achievements but for its honesty, its commitment to openness. Employees felt a deep connection to the organization's mission, a pride in its values, a trust in its leadership. They were not just employees; they were partners in a journey built on truth.

Nakka's legacy was not merely a culture of transparency but a belief—that trust was built on openness, that transparency was the foundation of connection. He had shown them that transparency was not a weakness but a strength, a commitment to respect and to trust.

Through his vision, Nakka had woven transparency into the heart of the organization, creating a culture where truth was honored, where trust was earned, a testament to the power of openness, to the courage to share.

Chapter 19

CONFLICT RESOLUTION – STRENGTHENING BONDS THROUGH UNDERSTANDING

Nakka's Philosophy: Conflict Is Not a Barrier, But a Bridge

Nakka had seen conflict in many forms—disagreements over ideas, misunderstandings among teams, clashes of values. He understood that in a complex organization, conflict was inevitable. But to him, conflict was not an obstacle to avoid; it was an opportunity, a way to strengthen relationships, to deepen understanding, to find truth in diversity. He believed that conflict, when met with patience and empathy, became a path to unity, to growth.

Conflict is not a division; it is a bridge, he thought. *It is an invitation to understand, to connect through honesty, to find common ground.*

For Nakka, conflict resolution was more than a skill; it was an act of respect, a commitment to truth and understanding. He believed that by approaching conflict openly, with a willingness to listen, the organization could transform disagreements into bonds, could create a culture where differences were celebrated, where unity was built through diversity.

A Conversation on Conflict with Radha, a Project Manager

One afternoon, Nakka met with Radha, a project manager who was known for her dedication but had recently faced tension with a colleague over a project decision. Radha was frustrated, feeling misunderstood, struggling to find a way forward.

"Radha," he asked gently, "what does conflict mean to you?"

She hesitated, her expression thoughtful. "I suppose… it feels like a barrier, like something that gets in the way of progress."

Nakka nodded, understanding her perspective. "But could conflict be more than that? Could it be a way to see differently, to learn, to grow closer?"

Radha looked at him, uncertain. "I hadn't thought of it that way. I've always seen it as… something to resolve, to move past."

"Conflict is a barrier only when we refuse to understand," Nakka replied, his voice steady. "But when we approach it with openness, it becomes a bridge, a way to deepen our understanding of others, to find shared purpose."

Radha listened, realizing now that conflict was not a hindrance but an opportunity, a way to build trust, to connect through respect and empathy.

Building Conflict Resolution as a Cultural Strength

Determined to make conflict resolution a pillar of the organization, Nakka introduced practices that encouraged open dialogue, empathy, and a commitment to understanding. He wanted conflict to be seen not as a disruption but as a chance to build unity, to strengthen relationships.

Steps to Create a Culture of Conflict Resolution:

1. **Conflict Resolution Training Focused on Empathy and Listening**
2. Nakka implemented training sessions that taught employees how to approach conflict with empathy, how to listen actively, how to seek understanding. These sessions fostered a culture where conflict resolution was not about winning but about connecting.
3. **Open Dialogue Spaces for Addressing Disagreements**
4. He created spaces where employees could address disagreements openly, where they could discuss differences without fear, without judgment. These dialogues became platforms for understanding, for finding common ground.

5. **Mediation Support to Guide Resolution**
6. Nakka introduced mediation support, a resource for employees who needed guidance in resolving conflicts. This support was not about imposing solutions but about facilitating understanding, about helping employees find their own paths to resolution.

A Philosophical Dialogue on Connection with Naveen, Head of Product Development

Nakka met with Naveen, the head of Product Development, a talented leader but often quick to defend his ideas, to resist disagreement. Nakka wanted him to see that connection was built not only through agreement but through understanding, that conflict could be a source of unity, of growth.

"Naveen," he asked, his tone thoughtful, "do you think connection is found only in agreement, or could it be strengthened through difference?"

Naveen looked at him, thoughtful. "I suppose... I've always thought unity came from shared views, from alignment."

"Alignment is important," Nakka replied, his gaze steady. "But true connection comes from understanding, from the willingness to see from another's perspective. Conflict is not a threat; it is an opportunity to build trust, to connect through difference."

Naveen listened, understanding now that conflict was not a challenge to his ideas but a chance to broaden them, to build a connection that was resilient, that honored both unity and diversity.

Embedding Conflict Resolution into the Organization's DNA

Nakka took steps to make conflict resolution a cultural standard, creating practices that approached conflict with respect, with empathy, with a commitment to understanding. He wanted conflict resolution to be a shared responsibility, a value that strengthened the organization's foundation.

Methods to Foster a Culture of Conflict Resolution:

1. **Weekly Reflection Circles for Open Dialogue**
2. Nakka introduced weekly reflection circles where employees could discuss challenges, disagreements, and concerns. These circles became spaces of honesty, of shared understanding, where conflict was addressed openly, respectfully.
3. **Collaborative Problem-Solving Workshops**
4. He established workshops focused on collaborative problem-solving, where teams worked through hypothetical conflicts, learning how to approach disagreements with empathy and openness. These workshops built a culture of connection, of unity through difference.
5. **Celebrating Resolution as a Success**
6. Nakka introduced the practice of celebrating successful conflict resolution, honoring teams and individuals who had approached disagreements with respect, who had turned conflict into connection. These celebrations reinforced the value of unity through understanding.

Philosophical Reflection: Conflict as a Path to Unity

In the stillness of his office, Nakka reflected on the nature of conflict, on its role as both challenge and opportunity. To him, conflict was not an end but a beginning, a path to unity that honored diversity, that built trust through truth.

Conflict is not a division; it is a chance to understand, he thought. *It is an invitation to connect, to see beyond ourselves, to find strength in difference.*

He believed that conflict, when met with respect, became a bridge, a way to deepen relationships, to build a culture where unity was not conformity but connection. In this belief, he found purpose—a purpose that guided his vision for an organization that saw conflict as a catalyst for growth.

The Impact of a Conflict-Resolution Culture

In the months that followed, Nakka saw the transformation within his teams. Employees approached conflict with openness, with a willingness to listen, to understand. The reflection circles, the mediation support, the collaborative workshops—all had nurtured a culture where conflict was not a disruption but a path to unity.

One day, he overheard Radha speaking to her team.

"Here, we don't avoid conflict. We address it, because every difference is a chance to connect."

Nakka felt a quiet pride. His vision had taken root. The organization had become a place where conflict was approached with empathy, where differences were honored, where unity was built through understanding.

Key Takeaways from Nakka's Approach to Conflict Resolution

1. **Conflict as a Bridge to Understanding**
2. Through empathy training and open dialogue, Nakka created a culture where conflict was not feared but approached with respect, as a bridge to connection.
3. **Connection Through Difference, Not Conformity**
4. Nakka's conversations with leaders like Naveen redefined conflict as a chance to understand, creating a culture where unity was found through diversity.
5. **Respect as the Foundation of Resolution**
6. The mediation support and reflection circles fostered a culture of respect, making conflict resolution a shared responsibility, a value of mutual understanding.
7. **Celebration of Resolution as a Source of Unity**
8. By honoring successful conflict resolution, Nakka reinforced the idea that unity was strengthened through understanding, through the courage to connect beyond disagreement.

Legacy of Nakka's Vision for Conflict Resolution

In the years that followed, the organization became known not only for its achievements but for its culture of unity, its commitment to understanding. Employees felt a deep connection to each other, a pride in their role as part of a community built on respect. They were not just colleagues; they were allies, bound by a commitment to truth, to connection.

Nakka's legacy was not merely a culture of conflict resolution but a belief—that conflict was not an obstacle but an opportunity, that unity was found in understanding. He had shown them that conflict was a bridge, a path to trust, to connection.

Through his vision, Nakka had woven conflict resolution into the heart of the organization, creating a culture where differences were honored, where unity was strengthened, a testament to the power of understanding, to the courage to connect.

Chapter 20

DECISION-MAKING – BALANCING VISION AND PRACTICALITY

Nakka's Principle: Decision-Making is the Art of Balancing Vision and Reality

Nakka believed that decision-making was more than a strategic exercise; it was a reflection of character, a practice that demanded both vision and restraint. He had seen leaders make bold choices that lacked grounding, as well as cautious decisions that missed opportunity. To him, effective decision-making required a delicate balance—a way of honoring both ideals and realities, an alignment of purpose with practicality.

Decision-making is not about certainty, he thought. *It is about courage, about choosing with clarity, about navigating complexity with purpose.*

For Nakka, every decision was an opportunity to strengthen the organization's path forward, to align its actions with its values. He believed that in each choice, a leader revealed their character, their vision, their commitment to serve both the organization's mission and its people.

A Conversation on Choice with Arjun, Head of Strategic Initiatives

One afternoon, Nakka sat with Arjun, the head of Strategic Initiatives, a leader known for his bold ideas but often criticized for taking risks that felt disconnected from the organization's current strengths. Arjun was passionate, driven, but Nakka sensed a need for balance, for a grounded approach to his vision.

"Arjun," he began, his voice calm, "what does decision-making mean to you?"

Arjun paused, thoughtful. "I suppose... it's about making bold moves, about pushing boundaries, about taking risks for the future."

Nakka nodded, recognizing his ambition. "But is decision-making only about vision? What of practicality, of understanding our present reality?"

Arjun looked at him, considering this. "I see the value in pragmatism, but... isn't it our job to push beyond what seems possible?"

"Yes, vision is essential," Nakka replied, his tone steady. "But vision without grounding becomes fantasy. True decision-making is not abandoning ambition but aligning it with reality, with purpose, with the courage to see both what could be and what is."

Arjun listened, understanding now that decision-making was not about risk alone but about discernment, a balance of inspiration and integrity.

Building Discernment as a Cultural Standard

Determined to make balanced decision-making a cultural strength, Nakka introduced practices that encouraged clarity, discernment, and the integration of both vision and practicality. He wanted decision-making to become not only a skill but a shared commitment to thoughtful, purposeful action.

Steps to Foster a Culture of Balanced Decision-Making:

1. **Decision-Making Frameworks for Strategic Clarity**
2. Nakka introduced frameworks that guided decision-making, helping teams evaluate both potential risks and opportunities. These frameworks encouraged teams to consider impact, feasibility, and alignment with the organization's mission, creating a culture of thoughtful choice.
3. **Risk Assessment Panels for Collaborative Insight**
4. He established risk assessment panels, where leaders from different departments gathered to discuss major decisions, to share insights,

to evaluate choices from multiple perspectives. These panels became spaces of collaboration, of balance between ambition and caution.

5. **Reflective Practice for Post-Decision Learning**
6. Nakka implemented reflective practice sessions, where teams reviewed past decisions, learning from both successes and missteps. These reflections deepened understanding, helping teams refine their approach to future choices.

A Philosophical Dialogue on Purpose with Neha, Director of Marketing

Nakka met with Neha, the Director of Marketing, a leader known for her meticulous planning but often hesitant to take bold action. Nakka wanted her to see that decision-making was not just about caution; it was about purpose, about trusting one's vision with clarity, with courage.

"Neha," he asked, his tone thoughtful, "do you think purpose is only found in safe choices, or could it be in daring decisions?"

Neha looked at him, thoughtful. "I suppose… I've always seen purpose as careful planning, as avoiding unnecessary risks."

"Purpose requires care, yes," Nakka replied, his gaze intent. "But it also requires courage, the willingness to step forward, to trust in vision. True decision-making is not fear but discernment, the ability to balance caution with boldness, purpose with practicality."

Neha listened, understanding now that decision-making was not a choice between risk and caution but an art of integration, a balance of vision and reality.

Embedding Discernment into the Organization's DNA

Nakka took steps to make balanced decision-making an integral part of the organization, creating practices that grounded vision in purpose, that balanced ambition with pragmatism. He wanted decision-making to be a shared strength, a value of discernment and clarity.

Methods to Normalize Discernment:

1. **Monthly Decision-Review Forums for Shared Learning**
2. Nakka introduced monthly forums where leaders reviewed significant decisions, discussing both their impact and alignment with the organization's mission. These forums became spaces of learning, reminders that decision-making was a shared journey.
3. **Scenario Planning Workshops for Vision and Practicality**
4. He implemented scenario planning workshops, where teams explored potential outcomes, learning to navigate complexity with both foresight and caution. These workshops fostered a culture of preparedness, of balanced vision.
5. **Celebrating Discernment as a Core Strength**
6. Nakka introduced an annual award for discernment, recognizing leaders who demonstrated balanced decision-making, who aligned vision with reality. This celebration honored discernment as a strength, a commitment to thoughtful choice.

Philosophical Reflection: Decision-Making as the Art of Balance

In the quiet moments of reflection, Nakka considered the nature of decision-making, of choice. To him, decision-making was not about certainty but about courage, a practice that aligned ideals with reality, purpose with practicality.

Decision-making is not about simplicity; it is about complexity, he thought. *It is the art of choosing with clarity, of balancing vision with the courage to see what is true.*

He believed that decision-making was not a formula but a journey, a path of discernment that honored both what could be and what was. In this belief, he found purpose—a purpose that guided his vision for an organization where decisions were made with integrity, with purpose, with balance.

The Impact of a Balanced Decision-Making Culture

In the months that followed, Nakka saw the transformation within his teams. Leaders approached decisions with clarity, with a willingness to balance ambition and caution. The decision-review forums, the risk assessment panels, the reflective practices—all had nurtured a culture where decision-making was not only strategic but grounded.

One day, he overheard Arjun speaking to his team.

"Here, we don't just act. We choose, with vision and with purpose."

Nakka felt a quiet pride. His vision had taken root. The organization had become a place where decision-making was not impulsive but thoughtful, where each choice was a reflection of shared purpose, of integrity.

Key Takeaways from Nakka's Approach to Decision-Making

1. **Decision-Making as a Reflection of Purpose**
2. Through frameworks and review forums, Nakka created a culture where decision-making was aligned with purpose, where choices were made with clarity and courage.
3. **Balance Between Vision and Practicality**
4. Nakka's conversations with leaders like Arjun redefined decision-making as the art of balance, creating a culture where vision was grounded in reality.
5. **Learning Through Reflection and Collaboration**
6. The risk assessment panels and reflective practices fostered a culture of learning, making decision-making a shared strength, a commitment to thoughtful action.
7. **Celebration of Discernment as a Core Value**
8. By honoring discernment, Nakka reinforced the idea that decision-making was not about risk alone but about balance, about the courage to choose with both heart and mind.

Legacy of Nakka's Vision for Decision-Making

In the years that followed, the organization became known not only for its achievements but for its clarity, its commitment to thoughtful choice. Employees felt a deep connection to the organization's mission, a pride in its values, a trust in its leaders. They were not just decision-makers; they were stewards of purpose, of integrity.

Nakka's legacy was not merely a culture of decision-making but a belief—that choice was an art, that vision and reality could align. He had shown them that decision-making was not a task but a commitment, a journey of balance, of clarity.

Through his vision, Nakka had woven discernment into the heart of the organization, creating a culture where decisions were made with purpose, with balance, a testament to the power of clarity, to the courage to choose.

Chapter 21

EMPLOYEE WELLNESS – PRIORITIZING WELL-BEING FOR SUSTAINED EXCELLENCE

Nakka's Belief: True Excellence Begins with Well-being

Nakka understood that an organization's strength lay in its people, that productivity, innovation, and commitment could only thrive in an environment that valued well-being. To him, employee wellness was more than an initiative—it was a philosophy, a testament to the organization's care for its people, a foundation that empowered individuals to give their best, to grow, to thrive.

Well-being is not a luxury, he thought. *It is a necessity, the root of true strength, the source of sustained excellence.*

For Nakka, wellness was not a program but a commitment, a way of honoring each person's humanity. He believed that by fostering an environment that supported physical, emotional, and mental health, the organization would not only increase its productivity but create a culture of respect, of loyalty, of shared purpose.

A Conversation on Wellness with Sanjay, Head of Operations

One day, Nakka met with Sanjay, the head of Operations, a leader known for his efficiency but often driven by a sense of urgency that overlooked rest, well-being. Sanjay was dedicated, focused, but Nakka sensed a need for balance, for a commitment to both performance and wellness.

"Sanjay," he asked gently, "what does wellness mean to you?"

Sanjay looked at him, thoughtful. "I suppose… it's important, but we have goals to meet, timelines to keep. Wellness can't always come first."

Nakka nodded, understanding the pressures of productivity. "But can productivity truly thrive without well-being? Can excellence be sustained if we do not value rest, if we do not care for our people?"

Sanjay hesitated, considering this. "I see the value in wellness, but… how do we balance it with the demands we face?"

"Wellness is not a distraction; it is an investment," Nakka replied, his tone steady. "True excellence is built on a foundation of well-being. If we want our people to give their best, we must first give them the space, the support, the care to be well."

Sanjay listened, realizing now that wellness was not a barrier to productivity but its foundation, that by valuing wellness, the organization strengthened its people, its purpose, its potential.

Integrating Wellness as a Cultural Pillar

Determined to make wellness a core value, Nakka introduced practices that nurtured physical, mental, and emotional health. He wanted wellness to be more than a policy; he wanted it to be a shared responsibility, a commitment to honoring each person's well-being.

Steps to Foster a Culture of Wellness:

1. **Flexible Work Policies for Balance and Care**
2. Nakka implemented flexible work policies, allowing employees to balance their personal needs with professional responsibilities. These policies gave employees control over their time, creating a culture where wellness was respected, where work supported life.
3. **Wellness Programs Focused on Holistic Health**
4. He introduced wellness programs that included physical fitness, mental health support, and stress management. These programs became resources of care, of strength, creating an environment where health was nurtured, where well-being was valued.

5. **Quiet Spaces for Rest and Reflection**
6. Nakka established quiet spaces within the office where employees could step away, recharge, find calm. These spaces became sanctuaries, reminders that wellness was a priority, a foundation for resilience and strength.

A Philosophical Dialogue on Balance with Deepa, Head of HR

Nakka met with Deepa, the head of HR, a leader who understood the value of wellness but often struggled to integrate it into the fast-paced environment of the organization. Nakka wanted her to see that wellness was not a secondary goal but a core commitment, a foundation of balance and strength.

"Deepa," he asked, his tone reflective, "do you think excellence is found only in work, or could it be in balance, in rest?"

Deepa looked at him, thoughtful. "I suppose… I've always thought productivity was the measure of success, that rest was something to fit around it."

"Productivity is important," Nakka replied, his gaze intent. "But true success is found in balance, in the care we give to ourselves, to our people. Wellness is not an interruption; it is a foundation. Without it, excellence is unsustainable."

Deepa listened, understanding now that wellness was not a distraction but a commitment, that balance was a source of strength, of lasting success.

Embedding Wellness into the Organization's DNA

Nakka took steps to make wellness an integral part of the organization, creating practices that supported physical, emotional, and mental health. He wanted wellness to be a shared responsibility, a value that strengthened the organization from within.

Methods to Normalize Wellness:

1. **Monthly Wellness Workshops and Check-Ins**
2. Nakka introduced monthly wellness workshops and check-ins, where employees could learn about health, mindfulness, and balance. These sessions became reminders that wellness was a shared commitment, a priority that was respected, supported.
3. **Mental Health Days and Support Networks**
4. He implemented mental health days, allowing employees to take time to recharge without stigma, without question. Support networks were established, creating a culture of openness, a safe space for discussing mental health.
5. **Celebrating Wellness as a Core Value**
6. Nakka introduced an annual wellness award, honoring individuals who demonstrated commitment to well-being, who encouraged balance and care within their teams. This celebration reinforced wellness as a strength, a value that honored each person's humanity.

Philosophical Reflection: Wellness as the Root of True Strength

In moments of solitude, Nakka reflected on the nature of wellness, on its role as both strength and foundation. To him, wellness was not an indulgence but a necessity, a path to excellence that honored each person's humanity, that strengthened the organization's foundation.

Well-being is not an expense; it is an investment, he thought. *It is the courage to care, to build strength through balance, to honor the people who give their best.*

He believed that wellness was the root of resilience, that true excellence began with well-being. In this belief, he found purpose—a purpose that guided his vision for an organization where wellness was honored, where people were valued, where strength was found in balance.

The Impact of a Wellness-Focused Culture

In the months that followed, Nakka saw the transformation within his teams. Employees approached work with energy, with balance, with a renewed sense of purpose. The flexible policies, the wellness programs, the quiet spaces—all had nurtured a culture where wellness was respected, where each person felt valued, supported.

One day, he overheard Sanjay speaking to his team.

"Here, we don't just work. We care—for ourselves, for each other, because wellness is our strength."

Nakka felt a quiet pride. His vision had taken root. The organization had become a place where wellness was prioritized, where excellence was built on a foundation of balance, of well-being.

Key Takeaways from Nakka's Approach to Wellness

1. **Wellness as the Foundation of Strength**
2. Through flexible policies and wellness programs, Nakka created a culture where well-being was prioritized, where productivity was built on balance.
3. **Balance Between Work and Life**
4. Nakka's conversations with leaders like Deepa redefined wellness as the source of resilience, creating a culture where work supported life, where people were honored.
5. **Care Through Openness and Support**
6. The mental health days and support networks fostered a culture of openness, making wellness a shared responsibility, a commitment to care.
7. **Celebration of Wellness as a Core Value**
8. By honoring wellness, Nakka reinforced the idea that excellence was found in balance, that well-being was the foundation of strength, of resilience.

Legacy of Nakka's Vision for Wellness

In the years that followed, the organization became known not only for its productivity but for its care, its commitment to well-being. Employees felt a deep connection to the organization's mission, a pride in its values, a trust in its leaders. They were not just workers; they were valued individuals, respected, honored.

Nakka's legacy was not merely a culture of wellness but a belief—that well-being was the foundation of strength, that true excellence began with care. He had shown them that wellness was not a luxury but a necessity, a commitment to humanity, to balance.

Through his vision, Nakka had woven wellness into the heart of the organization, creating a culture where well-being was prioritized, where strength was built on balance, a testament to the power of care, to the courage to honor each person.

Chapter 22

ETHICAL LEADERSHIP – LEADING WITH INTEGRITY AND PRINCIPLE

Nakka's Conviction: Leadership Without Integrity Is a Hollow Pursuit

For Nakka, leadership was not merely a position; it was a commitment, a responsibility that demanded the highest standards of integrity. He believed that ethical leadership was the foundation upon which trust, respect, and loyalty were built. To him, ethics were not just guidelines—they were principles, a compass that directed every decision, every action, every choice.

Integrity is not a rule; it is a commitment, he thought. *It is the courage to do what is right, even when it is difficult, even when it is unseen.*

Nakka understood that ethical leadership was more than transparency; it was a reflection of character, a dedication to principles that went beyond profit, beyond success. He believed that an organization led with integrity became a force for good, a source of trust and inspiration for its people and the world beyond.

A Conversation on Integrity with Kavita, Head of Finance

One afternoon, Nakka met with Kavita, the head of Finance, a leader known for her dedication to detail but sometimes faced with decisions where ethical lines could blur under pressure to meet financial goals. Kavita was skilled, precise, but Nakka sensed a need for clarity, for a commitment to integrity over convenience.

"Kavita," he asked gently, "what does integrity mean to you?"

Kavita hesitated, thoughtful. "I suppose… it's about being honest, about doing what's right, but sometimes… circumstances push us to make difficult choices."

Nakka nodded, understanding the challenges. "But can integrity be situational, something that changes with circumstances? Or is it a commitment that stands firm, even when it is hard?"

Kavita looked at him, considering his words. "I see your point. I've always tried to do what's right, but sometimes… we're tempted to compromise to reach targets, to meet expectations."

"Integrity is not about perfection," Nakka replied, his tone steady. "It is about principle. True leadership is not achieving at any cost; it is achieving with honor, with a commitment to truth. Ethics is the foundation of respect, of trust—it is what gives our success meaning."

Kavita listened, understanding now that integrity was not a restriction but a strength, a commitment to leading with honor, with courage.

Building Ethical Leadership as a Cultural Standard

Determined to make ethics a pillar of the organization, Nakka introduced practices that reinforced integrity, transparency, and a commitment to principle. He wanted ethical leadership to be more than a guideline; he wanted it to be a foundation, a shared commitment to doing what was right.

Steps to Foster a Culture of Ethical Leadership:

1. **Code of Ethics as a Living Document**
2. Nakka introduced a code of ethics that went beyond compliance. This document served as a moral compass, a guide for actions that honored integrity, that reminded everyone that ethics was a responsibility, a standard that the organization would not compromise.
3. **Ethics Committees for Accountability and Guidance**
4. He established ethics committees to support decision-making, to provide a space where ethical dilemmas could be discussed openly.

These committees became pillars of integrity, offering guidance and accountability, reinforcing the organization's commitment to principle.

5. **Leadership by Example – Modeling Integrity**
6. Nakka believed that ethical leadership began at the top. He encouraged leaders to model integrity in every decision, every action, every interaction. This standard became a beacon, a reminder that ethics was a commitment each leader upheld.

A Philosophical Dialogue on Principle with Suresh, Director of Sales

Nakka met with Suresh, the Director of Sales, a talented leader often caught between ambitious targets and ethical considerations. Nakka wanted him to see that principle was not an obstacle to success but the path to meaningful achievement, a commitment to doing what was right over what was easy.

"Suresh," he asked, his tone reflective, "do you believe success can be built on compromise, or could it be strengthened by principle?"

Suresh looked at him, thoughtful. "I suppose… I've always seen success as reaching goals, but sometimes… compromise feels necessary."

"Goals are important," Nakka replied, his gaze steady. "But true success is built on integrity, on a commitment to principle. Ethical leadership is not about shortcuts; it is about building something lasting, something honorable, something we can stand behind with pride."

Suresh listened, understanding now that ethics was not a barrier to achievement but a foundation of trust, that principle was a path to meaningful success.

Embedding Ethics into the Organization's DNA

Nakka took steps to make ethics an integral part of the organization, creating practices that strengthened integrity, that reinforced the organization's commitment to doing what was right. He wanted ethical leadership to be a shared strength, a value that honored both purpose and principle.

Methods to Normalize Ethical Leadership:

1. **Quarterly Ethics Roundtables for Open Dialogue**
2. Nakka introduced quarterly ethics roundtables, where employees could discuss ethical dilemmas, share insights, and learn from one another. These roundtables became spaces of trust, reminders that ethics was a shared commitment, a standard that everyone upheld.
3. **Ethics Training for Principled Decision-Making**
4. He implemented ethics training, teaching employees how to navigate complex situations with integrity, how to make principled choices. These trainings reinforced the organization's commitment to doing what was right.
5. **Celebrating Integrity as a Core Value**
6. Nakka introduced annual integrity awards, honoring individuals who exemplified ethical leadership, who demonstrated commitment to principle. This celebration reinforced ethics as a strength, a foundation of trust and respect.

Philosophical Reflection: Ethics as the Soul of Leadership

In the stillness of his office, Nakka reflected on the nature of ethics, on its role as both standard and foundation. To him, ethics was not a guideline but a commitment, a dedication to doing what was right, to leading with honor, with integrity.

Ethics is not a restriction; it is a foundation, he thought. *It is the courage to choose principle over convenience, to lead with respect, to honor the trust we are given.*

He believed that ethical leadership was not about what was achieved but how it was achieved, that true success was built on integrity, on principle. In this belief, he found purpose—a purpose that guided his vision for an organization where ethics was honored, where integrity was a standard.

The Impact of an Ethical Leadership Culture

In the months that followed, Nakka saw the transformation within his teams. Leaders approached decisions with integrity, with a commitment to doing what was right. The ethics committees, the code of ethics, the roundtables—all had nurtured a culture where ethics was respected, where each person felt a responsibility to lead with honor.

One day, he overheard Kavita speaking to her team.

"Here, we don't just achieve. We honor integrity, because ethics is our strength."

Nakka felt a quiet pride. His vision had taken root. The organization had become a place where ethics was not only a policy but a principle, where integrity was the foundation of every decision, of every achievement.

Key Takeaways from Nakka's Approach to Ethical Leadership

1. **Ethics as the Foundation of Trust and Respect**
2. Through the code of ethics and ethics committees, Nakka created a culture where ethical leadership was a shared commitment, a standard of integrity.
3. **Integrity as a Path to Meaningful Success**
4. Nakka's conversations with leaders like Suresh redefined ethics as a source of strength, creating a culture where success was built on principle, on honor.
5. **Accountability Through Open Dialogue**
6. The ethics roundtables and training sessions fostered a culture of accountability, making ethical leadership a shared responsibility, a commitment to respect and trust.
7. **Celebration of Integrity as a Core Strength**
8. By honoring ethical leadership, Nakka reinforced the idea that integrity was not a choice but a commitment, a foundation of meaningful achievement.

Legacy of Nakka's Vision for Ethical Leadership

In the years that followed, the organization became known not only for its achievements but for its integrity, its commitment to ethical leadership. Employees felt a deep connection to the organization's mission, a pride in its values, a trust in its leaders. They were not just achievers; they were stewards of principle, of respect.

Nakka's legacy was not merely a culture of ethical leadership but a belief—that true success was built on integrity, that leadership was a commitment to doing what was right. He had shown them that ethics was not a restriction but a foundation, a testament to honor, to principle.

Through his vision, Nakka had woven ethics into the heart of the organization, creating a culture where integrity was honored, where success was built on principle, a testament to the power of respect, to the courage to lead with honor.

Conclusion

THE LEGACY OF VISION AND INTEGRITY

Nakka's Final Reflection: Building Something That Lasts

As Nakka stood at the heart of the organization he had helped shape, he felt a quiet sense of fulfillment. The journey had not been easy; it had required resilience, commitment, and a belief that values were not just words but the very foundation of success. Nakka understood that leadership was not about control but about influence, about guiding others through vision, through integrity, through a commitment to doing what was right.

Legacy is not built in actions alone, he thought. *It is built in principles, in the courage to stand by what we believe, in the lives we touch, in the trust we build.*

For Nakka, the legacy he left was not in policies or processes but in the people he had inspired, in the culture he had fostered. He believed that true leadership lived on in the hearts of those who shared his vision, who carried his values forward, who saw leadership not as a title but as a purpose.

A Conversation with Priya, a Young Leader Inspired by Nakka's Journey

One day, as Nakka walked through the office, he was approached by Priya, a young leader who had recently taken on a management role. She looked up to him, inspired by his journey, by the principles he embodied. She wanted to understand, to learn from his wisdom, to carry forward his legacy.

"Nakka," she began, her voice filled with admiration, "what would you say is the most important lesson in leadership?"

Nakka looked at her, his gaze thoughtful. "Leadership," he replied, "is not about authority. It is about responsibility, about serving a purpose greater than oneself. It is about integrity, about the courage to lead with honor."

Priya listened, her eyes bright with understanding. "And how do you know if you've made a difference?"

"We make a difference," Nakka said gently, "when we inspire others to carry forward what we believe, when we build something that lasts, not in results alone but in values, in trust. Legacy is not what we achieve; it is the principles we leave behind."

Priya nodded, feeling the weight of his words, understanding that leadership was not about power but about purpose, about leaving a legacy of respect, of integrity.

The Enduring Principles of Nakka's Leadership

In the years to come, the organization would carry forward the principles that Nakka had so deeply embedded within its culture. His commitment to clarity, integrity, wellness, and ethical leadership would live on, guiding future leaders, inspiring each employee to contribute their best.

Key Lessons from Nakka's Journey:

1. **Integrity as the Heart of Leadership**
2. Nakka's commitment to integrity became a standard that the organization honored. His belief that ethical leadership was the foundation of trust created a culture where honesty was respected, where success was built on principles that would not waver.
3. **Clarity and Vision as a Guide**
4. Nakka's vision brought clarity, his sense of purpose guiding every decision, every action. Future leaders would remember that clarity was not about simplicity but about focus, about aligning actions with values.

5. **Commitment to Well-being as Strength**
6. Nakka's emphasis on wellness redefined the organization's view of productivity. He showed them that well-being was not a luxury but a foundation, a source of resilience and strength that allowed people to thrive.
7. **Ethics as a Legacy of Trust**
8. By making ethics a cultural pillar, Nakka left behind a legacy of trust, a commitment to honor, to respect. His belief in ethical leadership would continue to inspire, reminding future leaders that integrity was the foundation of true success.

Nakka's Final Reflection: Legacy as a Shared Responsibility

As he prepared to leave, Nakka felt a quiet sense of purpose. He knew that his legacy would not be carried by him alone but by each person who believed in his vision, who honored the values he had instilled. He had built something that could last, not because of structure alone but because of the trust, the commitment, the principles he had woven into the fabric of the organization.

Legacy is not what we leave; it is what we live, he thought. *It is the commitment to purpose, the courage to honor integrity, the choice to lead with heart.*

He believed that the organization was more than a collection of individuals; it was a community bound by shared values, by a commitment to doing what was right. In this belief, he found fulfillment—a fulfillment that came not from his achievements but from the lives he had touched, the trust he had built.

A Final Message to the Organization

Before leaving, Nakka addressed the organization one last time. His words were simple, filled with the wisdom of a journey completed, a legacy begun.

"Thank you for believing in this vision, for honoring these values, for sharing in this journey. Remember, leadership is not about power but about purpose. Carry forward this commitment, this trust. Build with integrity, lead with heart, and you will create something that lasts."

The room was silent, filled with a quiet respect. Each person felt the weight of his words, understood the gift of his legacy, the strength of his commitment to them, to the organization, to a purpose that would continue long after he was gone.

A Legacy of Integrity, Vision, and Purpose

As Nakka walked away from the organization he had helped build, he felt a profound sense of peace. He knew that his legacy would endure, that the values he had championed would live on, that his vision would continue to guide, to inspire. He had shown them that leadership was not about what was achieved but about how it was achieved, that true success was built on integrity, on purpose.

Nakka's journey was not an end; it was a beginning, a legacy of leadership that would shape the organization for generations to come. He had left them not just with policies, with practices, but with principles, with a commitment to honor, to integrity.

Through his vision, Nakka had woven a legacy that would not fade, a testament to the power of purpose, to the courage to lead with heart. He had shown them that leadership was not a destination but a journey, a path walked with honor, with respect, with the belief that true greatness lay not in success alone but in the values that endured.